God's Rainbow

and

My Dream

A Slice of Life

Mary C. Cape-Juarez

authorHOUSE™

1663 LIBERTY DRIVE, SUITE 200
BLOOMINGTON, INDIANA 47403
(800) 839-8640
WWW.AUTHORHOUSE.COM

First published by AuthorHouse 12/02/05

ISBN: 1-4208-8790-4 (sc)
ISBN: 1-4208-8791-2 (dj)

Library of Congress Control Number: 2005909137

Printed in the United States of America
Bloomington, Indiana

This book is printed on acid-free paper.

Scriptures were taken from the Saint Joseph Edition of THE NEW AMERICAN BIBLE

Dedication

This book is dedicated to my Lord and Savior Jesus Christ, and to His Heavenly Father for giving me the words to share with so many people. I praise Him for everything He has helped me with to be able to make this dream come true. When I see His miraculous rainbow up in His peaceful blue sky, I know that He is there with me, taking my hand and leading me on this faithful journey.

I want to thank my biological mother, because if she had not decided to give birth to me, and to place me for adoption, I would not be where I am today.

I want to thank my parents, Virginia and Cletus "Hinie" Cape, for all of the love and support they gave to me throughout my life, but more importantly for raising me in God's love and His graces. I thank them for teaching me of His peace and joy that He waits so patiently to fill my heart with. I am who I am, because of my mother and father's love and their spiritual guidance throughout my entire life. My mother and father are both in Heaven now, but I know as I write this book, they look down upon me smiling, and I can feel their presence within my heart. It was my mother's dream for me to write a book someday with all of the words that God had given me. When God called her home, her dream then became my dream. My father was able to watch me write over half of this book before his time on earth was over. I'm sure he sent me lots of help to finish it.

A special thanks to my dear Aunt Helen, who prayed constantly for this book to be written, but who also did not live long enough to see it accomplished. I'm sure when she went to Heaven; she personally went before the Lord with her prayers.

There are so many friends who have encouraged me with their support for my vision, and because of them, I have found the courage to step forward and to pursue this dream.

I thank God for blessing me with my beautiful children, Christie, Marjoe, and Ian, who always gave me a reason to keep going when sometimes I felt like giving up. They offered their support when I needed encouragement and laughter at times when my heart was full of sadness. They gave me band aids of love to cover my broken spirits.

I thank God for blessing me with my loving and dedicated husband Victor, who taught me to love again when I thought my broken heart would never heal, and who made the decision to go to church with me on that first date instead of waiting until I got home to pick me up. God knew how long my heart had ached to share His love with someone special. Shawn and Crystal, my two step daughters, have also been there to encourage me on this journey.

I thank Father Tom for his wisdom and inspiration that helped to encourage me in writing this book and his kind words that helped make this book a dream come true.

There are many names mentioned in this book who have given me permission to share a part of their lives with you. Thank you for allowing me to share how God has worked in your life.

I thank God for His patience with me throughout these years when I had no idea how to even begin with this book. I thank Him for the storms in my life which have brought about many rainbows that always reminded me of His promise to me.

May God bless each and every one of you, who have helped me on this journey. May you always know how much I love you and appreciate your loving encouragement and inspiration.

"Sometimes in life we have to walk through the worst of storms in order to see the most colorful rainbows."

Table of Contents

Dedication   *v*
Acknowledgements   *x*
Our Journey In Life   *xi*

My Beginning   1
David   7
A Lifetime Of Friends   13
Time Is Precious   23
A New Journey Traveled   31
My Mothers' Love   57
My Father's Love   69
The Family That Prays Together   75
Lord, Bless My Child   83
A Lifetime Of Faith   93
A Journey To Heaven   101
Another Goodbye   109
When God Speaks   121
The End Of The Rainbow   133

Prayer For Forgiveness   *140*
Prayer For Guidance   *141*
Prayer To Do Your Will   *142*
"Thank You" Prayer   *143*

On April 8, 2003, as I sat in my car in the parking lot at the factory where I worked, I started feeling the urge very strongly about writing this book. I always drove to work early enough to sit and pray before I went inside. I would sit in my car and wish that I was doing something else in my life besides working in a factory. These words came to my mind that particular morning almost faster than I could write them down.

Dear Heavenly Father

It is my dream to publish a book that will glorify Your name, and bring hearts and souls even closer to You. If it is Your will, then please show me the path to take to help make my dream come true, lead me to the people who can help, and encourage me as I travel this journey, never letting me grow weary. Please take my hand and show me the way, in Jesus' name, I pray. Amen.

JOHN 16:23

"AMEN, AMEN, I SAY TO YOU, WHATEVER YOU ASK THE FATHER IN MY NAME HE WILL GIVE YOU."

I knew, then, that it was the prayer that I needed to start praying every morning if I truly wanted to do God's will. When I read it to my dear Aunt Helen, she wanted me to make a copy for her so she could start praying it everyday too, in hopes that double prayers would get the job finished quicker. After she passed away, I found the copy on her telephone desk. I'm sure she had prayed it every morning for me.

Each chapter of this book holds a cherished memory of someone very special. The end of each chapter has a scripture to reveal to us how Christ's words back then can relate to our own lives now. I wrote a reflection in hopes that you will take time to think of someone who has touched your heart in the same way that someone touched mine. A prayer ends each chapter to thank God for our blessings and to pray for one another.

Acknowledgements

My heartfelt thanks and deepest gratitude to:

AuthorHouse, for publishing the dream in my heart.

Father Tom Oedy, for his encouraging words when this book was only a dream, and for his encouraging "review" of my book after he finished reading it.

Sister Rozanne, Jodi, and Donita, for their help in answering all of the computer and grammar questions I had so many different times.

Laurie, a dear friend who contributed endless hours sitting at my computer, as I watched in amazement at all she was capable of doing at this incredible machine that I was so unsure of. Everytime I called her and screamed "Help!" she was there for me.

Mrs. Melinda Jones, for proof reading and giving me her time at such a busy time in her own life.

Mr. Richard Smith, "Smitty", (who happened to be everyone's favorite English teacher) for all of the proofreading, editing and corrections, but especially for the advice he gave me, that I know God wanted him to share with me.

Denise Tressler, who recently published a book herself and wanted to unselfishly share the knowledge that she had gained through her own experience.

Diane, for always reminding me that "It'll be O.K."

Prayer Warriors, You are all awesome! I could not have done this without you! As Pauline always said, **"WITH GOD ALL THINGS ARE POSSIBLE"** <u>MATTHEW 19:26</u>

Our Journey In Life

Our lives began as a journey many years ago. We all began this journey not knowing where we would be going, or how we would even get there. For some, God was a part of our lives from the beginning, for others, He was not. We've all made mistakes along our life's path, we have all sinned, and we have all stumbled and fallen; but God was always there walking along beside of us to pick us back up, even if we weren't aware of it. The mistakes we have made, the relationships that have been severed, and the hearts that were broken along the way don't matter anymore. What does matter is that Christ died for our sins to free us. God gave His only Son and that is what matters to us now. He forgives us, and He loves us unconditionally for all eternity.

God has brought us all together for a special reason. He picked us out, one by one, and brought our hearts and souls together so that we might travel our journey together. We have learned from our sins, we have been strengthened by our mistakes, and we have grown more compassionate through our tragedies and sorrows. We have been bonded together by our Heavenly Father who only wants us to love Him and to share His word with others. He has forgiven us for our mistakes, and now He wants us to forgive ourselves, as He continues to remind us of His love and peace that He so willingly gives to us.

God brought us together in order for us to walk hand in hand, to help each other heal our past, to bring about a spiritual renewal inside of our deepest being, and to help each other laugh and cry together. He has bonded us to show us a deeper meaning of the word friendship.

As He gives us the sun to warm our hearts, let us give our warmth to someone who is lonely. As He gives us His gentle rain falling upon the earth, let us shower someone with a message they have never heard, and as His full moon guides us in the darkest of the night, let His light shine through us into someone's life who feels hopeless right now.

Our God is awesome, His work is marvelous. He has bonded our lives spiritually and He is waiting for us to take each other's hands and begin our new journey together. With God as our guide, there's no end to how many miles we can travel, how many hearts we can touch along the way, and how many searching souls we can begin to lead back to Him. This will be a journey we will never forget.

My Beginning

I sit here at my little kitchen table, trying to look out to see over our huge back yard which ends at the riverbank. I can hear the birds softly singing, "Good Morning everyone," but yet I cannot see them because the fog lies heavily in the air, but I know that they are close. I wonder, "Where would I be right now if I did not have God in my life?" I answer to myself that I do not know, I can't imagine. I feel like my life has been like this foggy morning, I may not have been able to see too far ahead which put a fear inside my heart, but then somewhere out of the depths of the air, I could hear God's voice quietly whispering to me, "I am here." Unseen, like the birds are today, but ever so present in my thoughts, He is there.

I hear a train in the background, and it disrupts my quiet thoughts. I will be going to church soon to thank our Heavenly Father for being ever so present in my life, and for forgiving me for the times when I was not as present in His. I ponder at the thought that God really has been in my life since the beginning.

My life began on June 20, 1953 in Cleveland, Ohio. I was born to a single mother who was 20 years old at the time of my birth. I do not know the circumstances in her life, and I may never know them, but I do know that God must have been present in her life whether she was aware of Him or not. She gave to me the most precious gift of life, as I'm sure God wanted her to do.

In those five months after my birth, she must have desperately and secretly tried so hard to make her decision about me. In November of that same year she had her answer, she signed the adoption papers.

God chose to take that time and search the world over to find the perfect parents for me. He finally found them here in this little farming community in Edgerton, Ohio. It was then that my biological mother would give to me her second most precious gift. She gave me up for adoption so that I could have a better life then what she could give me. I was given the gift of two loving and caring people who would become my parents. God chose Virginia and Cletus "Hinie" Cape to be the parents that would raise me as their very own child.

I remember my mother telling me as I was growing up that when they went to Cleveland to see me for the first time, she saw my long legs and told my dad that I was to be their daughter. My mom was always rather short, 5'0", and spent most of her life climbing up on foot stools to reach things she couldn't get to on her own. We often laughed about that as I grew up to my 5'6 ½.

The trip to bring me home was a challenging one due to a severe snowstorm that day. It is about a 3 ½ hour trip now; I can only imagine what it would have been like over fifty years ago. When my mother and father made it back to Edgerton that day, they stopped uptown to our little town's friendly restaurant. My dad went in to get the girls to tell them to come out to the car. I guess he and my mom wanted to show me off. I was reminded of this story when my mother passed away ten years ago. A lady that was working that day back in February of 1954 shared this story to remind me of how proud my parents were the day they brought me home.

I was greeted home that cold snowy day by a 1 ½ year old brother, Steve, whom they had adopted a year earlier. My life began to unfold on that eighty acre farm out in the country. God's love was so obvious while I was growing up. I would witness the sun coming up behind our big barn, and then setting across the corn fields every night. I was raised in a Catholic home, a very simple and modest farm house which held so much love and joy that I never needed anything else. Life was so simple back then in those times. Dad farmed those eighty acres, and also worked in a factory later on in his life. Mom was home each day sewing my outfits and taking care of our home. I attended St. Mary's Catholic School through eighth grade, where I went to

Mass everyday as soon as we would get off the school bus. Of course, on the weekends, we would also attend Mass.

You can see why God was so much a part of my life from the beginning. I don't think a day ever started nor ended without God's name being mentioned. I wrote a poem years ago which I'd like to share with you. It truly tells the story of how God came to be such an important part of my life.

My Parents' Friend

One time when I was very young
My parents said to me,
"We want you to meet a friend of ours
Let's go and you will see."

They took me to his beautiful house
Which took my breath away,
They told me that their friend would be
Beside me everyday.

I was too young to understand
But each day as life went on,
I realized that their friend was there
To guide and lead me on.

He helped me smile when I was down
He took my clouds away,
He promised if I held his hand
We'd be together everyday.

Well that was many years ago
And one thing that is odd,
I never heard their friend's last name
I only know him as "God".

The gift of faith that my parents gave to me was the best gift I ever received. I have never outgrown it, and it has never worn out. It becomes more valuable as the years pass by. Even when I chose not to fully use it, it was still there. The gift of faith, the love of God, and the incredible sense of knowing that I would be nothing without Him in my life, is in fact the greatest gift that parents can ever give their children. I have thanked them for this gift over and over again. I know they gave it to me out of their love for God, because He had always been there for them, and they wanted me too, to have that security that only our Heavenly Father can give. My mother and father are both in Heaven now, but I know they still hear me saying, "Thank You."

I look back over my life and wonder where I would be now if I did not have God as the foundation for everything my life stood for. Who would I be? What would I be doing? The answers are unknown. I know how fortunate I am for what I have had. I know that I pray for those people out there who have not had the opportunity to welcome God into their lives as I have had.

I think that growing up in this small community and being raised in the country was an opportunity in itself. I was raised on a farm helping my dad with chores in the barn. Seeing baby pigs and calves being born, and watching God's miraculous hand at work in giving the gift of life, was a regular experience for me. While living in the country, and witnessing a dark summers night hold enough stars to actually cover the sky, gave me a real sense of God's presence. I still remember sitting out back, and the full moon would shine across those fields giving a shadowy outline of all of God's creations.

About a ½ mile down the road from our house was a little woods where my brother Steve and I would walk to in the summer. I can remember those little purple flowers that covered the ground beside the small tiny pond in the woods. There would be little tadpoles swimming all over as we picked as many flowers as our hands could hold. As we would walk back home to give mom her special bouquet, we would be dropping them all along the way. She would get so excited when we would present her with our gift.

The only sounds we would hear when we went to bed were the dogs barking, and of course the crickets would be singing their own special melody. Off in the distant, two miles down the road, I would hear the faint sound of a train whistle. I would awaken to the birds singing, the cows mooing, and the sun shining brightly in my bedroom window. It was so much God's land with God's creatures surrounding me. It was a peaceful setting with a million twinkling stars winking at me. It made me believe that God was surely watching me to see if I was aware of the beauty that He had given to me.

This was the life that I came to know God, to honor Him, and to thank Him for all of His beautiful creations that He gave to me to enjoy. I always wondered how anyone could look up at that beautiful full moon that appeared so mysterious, and ever doubt that there was someone up there more powerful than anyone here on earth. I was blessed by having God surround me throughout my childhood.

I saw my parents turn to Him for guidance and support. I heard them thank Him for our family, our food, our farm, and for everything that we had been blessed with. We were so rich in so many different ways, but not rich in the same meaning of rich today. I look back on those quiet happy family times, and I realize now that we had everything we needed, and much more. We had God's love, and my parents gave me the seed of faith that they planted when I was a baby. God was already nurturing that seed turning it into a foundation of hope for my future.

During my high school years, I started writing poems often. I remember sitting in study hall and writing poems about the Vietnam War when it was going on. I would write my thoughts down, clearing myself of so many questions, but never really finding a place to put them. I guess I never realized back then that God had actually blessed me with a talent for writing and expressing my thoughts so easily.

Never did I dream back then that someday I would be writing this book. God knew even then that eventually I would come to realize this precious gift, and I would share it with my own little town first, and then the rest of the world. This takes me into my next chapter to tell how I came to realize that I needed to start hanging on to these words that God was giving to me.

JEREMIAH 29:11

"FOR I KNOW WELL THE PLANS I HAVE IN MIND FOR YOU, SAYS THE LORD. PLANS FOR YOUR WELFARE, NOT FOR WOE! PLANS TO GIVE YOU A FUTURE FULL OF HOPE."

REFLECTION:

God wanted you to hear about His love and faithfulness. Is there someone you could thank today who planted the seed of faith in you, or that nutured that seed so your life could have meaning and purpose? What does He have planned for your life?

Dear Heavenly Father

I thank You for the life that You have given me. I praise You for giving me parents who showed me Your love and faithfulness. They planted a seed of faith that grew into a field of hope. I pray for all those children who did not have the same peaceful life that I was blessed with. Please give to them a feeling of encouragement and send someone to them to teach them of Your love. In the most precious name of Your Son, Jesus Christ. Amen.

David

When I was growing up in the country, all of us neighbors were like family. We helped each other out if someone was sick. Volunteers would come in to farm the crops if something happened that left it impossible for someone to do it themselves. People were not only neighbors, but they were truly friends watching out for one another.

There was a family that lived a mile down the road from us. They were Marvin and Janie Dietsch, and they were the most loving and caring family. They had five beautiful children, Greg, Michelle, Eric, David, and Natalie. I babysat for the chlldren at different times when Janie and Marvin would go away. In the spring of my senior year, my parents decided to sell the farm and move into town. Both Steve and I were graduating. Steve was getting married after graduation, and mom and dad decided they didn't need to hold on to this big old farm house. So in May that year, we sold the farm and the house, and moved into town. I felt like my whole life was coming to an end. I really hated to leave the country and the peaceful serenity that I had grown to love, but of course I wasn't ready to be on my own, so I went with my parents.

After living in town, and being away from all of our neighbors for years, I eventually lost contact with many of them. The Dietsches were one of those families that I didn't see as much of, but when we did, it seemed we had never really ever lost contact with them. As strange as it seemed, after my brother married, he and his wife ended up renting their first apartment from the Dietsches, which was right down the road from where we lived before.

I too, eventually married and didn't see too many of my past country neighbors at all. My mom and dad still kept in touch with most of them, and especially Janie and Marvin. I always looked at them as a true family of God. They raised their children in the same way my parents had, with the love of God, and daily thanking Him for blessings upon their family.

Then the true test of their faith came, a day in their lives when the sun quit shining and the clouds appeared in the sky creating a dark, gray cast upon their lives. Their thirteen year old son David was riding his bike ½ mile from his house when a car came up over the hill. The driver was not able to see David, and the accident happened. David lost his life to that accident.

I was twenty-nine years old at the time, with three children of my own. I was not one to go to the funeral home unless I actually had to. When I was growing up, it used to terrify me, but then my parents would tell me how much it meant to families when people would go and pay their respect for a loved one who had passed away. My parents asked me if I would want to go with them to the funeral home that warm fall day in October of 1982. The accident had happened on October 7, and this was just a few days later.

I told them I would go with them, but my heart just kept asking God, "Why?" as I stood at David's casket. A beautiful, blond haired child of God who had been taken so early from this earth was so hard to understand. I saw the pain in his family's eyes, and I just couldn't understand why any family as special as they were, would have to endure this much pain and grief. It made me question so many things. My heart was breaking in a million pieces over the innocent life that I had babysat for in earlier years. He had not even had the chance of living.

After we left the funeral home and my parents took me back to my house, I went in and quickly grabbed a pen and paper and a blanket, and I went outside to sit quietly under the warm, fall sun. A soft wind brushed against my cheek drying my tears as they fell. I remember as if it was yesterday. I looked up into the blue sky which held so much serenity, and once again asked God why someone so young and with so much to offer had to leave at such an early time in his life. I also asked Him why would a family as loving and caring as they were have to go through something this tragic. I knew how faithful they had always been to God, and it made me ask so many questions.

This time, unlike when I was asking in the funeral home, I heard God whispering to me these words. It ended up being the poem that I would give to Janie and Marvin as my gift to them.

David

A few days ago, God chose to come
And take your hand and lead you on,
We can't understand why you had to go
God has His reasons, this much we know.

He must have come for you in this early day
Knowing the road ahead, you wouldn't want to stay,
Maybe He could have seen the pain that layed ahead
And knew you didn't deserve it, so He'd take you now instead.

You were born into a family, so sweet and dear
And though you've left them, they'll always be near,
You felt so much love in this short time
More than some children in an entire lifetime.

A family you were blessed with that cared so much
And loved you dearly with every single touch,
Your brothers and sisters looked after you
In every single thing that you would do.

So though you weren't able to stay very long
You learned about love and happy songs,
The sun touched your hair and made it glisten
We can't ask questions now, we only must listen.

> *Someday we'll understand why all this took place*
> *And why we were left with such a sad space,*
> *But until that day comes, God will always be with you*
> *Your smile remaining in our hearts, till we can be there too.*

As I sat on my blanket writing these words as quickly as what God was giving them to me, my heart cried and cried. I sensed his parents' pain over their loss, but I also felt some relief in knowing that this special child of theirs was actually with God now. He was taken from their sight here, and from his earthly home, but was never far from his family's thoughts. I knew that he would live in their hearts forever, and yet the faith that my mother and father had raised me with reassured me that we would all see him again someday.

I continued to sit in the sunshine, savoring the peace that it brought into my heart. I went in to call my mother a little later to read her the words that God had just given to me. She paused quietly when I finished. I knew she was crying. In a quiet voice she said, "You have to share that with Janie and her family. They need to hear it."

I tried to tell her that I had been asking God, "why?" when He started giving me all those words. She reassured me that God had given me those words to share. I took her advice and rewrote the poem nicely. I mailed it out to them a few days later.

As I read back over my journal from that time in my life, I remember the struggles I dealt with in wondering why something like this had to happen.

Thurs. Oct. 7, '82 David Dietsch got killed on a bicycle tonight. God, I couldn't believe it! The Lord help them all!

Sun. Oct. 9, '82 Mom, Dad, and I went to the funeral home to see David. It's so hard to understand. I came home and sat outside and wrote a poem for David.

Thurs. Oct. 14, '82 Tonight, Janie Dietsch called to thank me for the poem. She said it had given them so much strength. I really felt something very spiritual and emotional. I couldn't believe it! It was a very satisfying feeling.

Now I look back and I realize that the "very spiritual and emotional" feeling that I was having was actually the Holy Spirit working inside of me. I remember the goose bumps when I talked to Janie that night, and the tears that we cried together over the phone. I just did not fully understand what was actually taking place. God had used me to help bring strength to their family during this time of sorrow, and God was using Janie to help me realize that He had given me a special gift that I should be sharing with other people.

I can still remember hanging up the phone that night, and as I stood in my kitchen, I just sobbed when I realized that God had used me in this manner. I called my mother to let her know what Janie had said and she reassured me that is what she had been trying to tell me all along.

It was that night in October of 1982, when I came to the decision of keeping all the words that God would ever give to me again. It was then that I knew I needed to continue to share these thoughts with the people I loved and cared about. It was at that moment when I truly felt like maybe I could make a difference in someone's life.

God was ever so present in that time of sorrow for Janie and Marvin and their entire family. I witnessed Him bringing them strength. I witnessed Him showering them with many friends and neighbors to help them out and to be a source of encouragement. As I look back now, I know that God was also drawing them into an even deeper relationship with Him. They depended on Him for their comfort and hope, and He was there for them, just as He had always been in the past. I learned a lot from that family in those years, and they are probably not even aware of it today.

When you see a family go through an unexpected tragedy as they did, I guess you realize that they can become closer to God, and become more compassionate towards others going through similar situations; or they can draw away from God entirely, and hold bitterness in their hearts. The Dietsches grew even closer to God, and He filled their hearts with peace.

MATTHEW 5:4

"BLESSED ARE THEY WHO MOURN, FOR THEY WILL BE COMFORTED."

REFLECTION:

Someone you know may have just lost someone who they loved very much. Is there anything you can do to help them through this time of sorrow?

Dear Heavenly Father

Thank you for allowing me to be a part of such a special family. I praise You for helping me to find words of comfort at such a sorrowful time in their life. Help me to always be a compassionate person towards those who are hurting. Remind me to always pray for those in need, so that my prayers will bring them much needed strength at a time when they feel so weak. In the most precious name of Your Son, Jesus Christ. Amen.

A Lifetime Of Friends

Looking back over the years, it is so obvious now that God really does send you friends during your entire life. Sometimes, I can't help but wonder why I haven't heard from someone in a long time. And then I realize that they were here at a certain time in my life, because God was using them to fulfill His purpose of getting me through a difficult time that I could not have survived on my own.

Growing up in the country, I had no choice but to have more "boy" friends then "girl" friends. The country seemed to have a much higher rate of boys than girls. Since my brother was only a year older than I was, there were always more guys around playing. I learned to swing on a rope in the barn from one side to the other and then jump in a pile of hay. Now I am scared of heights. A lot of things seem to change when you get older.

I played many games of baseball outside in the summer with our neighborhood team. I don't want to brag, but I really did put up a mean competition for the boys. My dad always told me that I could hit a ball just as far as any of the guys. I remember the excitement of the bat in my hands as I would step up to home plate. It was just as if I could hardly wait to prove myself to anyone who had doubts about a girl playing ball. I can still remember my dad laughing when I would hit a homerun, and the guys would be just staring at me as I would proudly round the bases heading for homeplate with my arms waving in the air. Our big barn held many a "free throwing" contest under the basketball hoop. Again, I showed them that a girl could make as many baskets as what any of the guys could. I wonder how many games of PIG we actually played in that barn during the time that I was growing up.

My neighbors down the road did have girls, so when I went to their house we would usually play Barbies. After they would mow their lawn (there were no riding mowers yet either), we would rake all the freshly cut grass together in big piles, and then make rows of grass creating different size squares, turning it into a house with a lot of rooms for our dolls to live in. We would spend hours outside on a hot summer's day pretending to live in those houses. There was no air conditioning in homes at that time, so sitting outside back then was feeling comfort when a fresh breeze would blow through our hair.

I don't really remember how many dolls we actually had, but I'm sure it wasn't many. Back then it didn't matter how much you had, it was just how much fun you could have with what you did have. Someones not having a lot just meant that the other children would share more of theirs. That's how it was back then. Those were the days when we would ride bikes to each other's houses, play for hours outside doing nothing, and be content with whatever we could find to do. It was an innocent time, and there were many friends among the neighborhood.

Those were the days when I now look back and realize that those children I played with for so many years would become my "childhood friends." They would eventually become a happy memory to be cherished in my heart forever. Those were the friends who made me laugh, and would watch "The Mickey Mouse Club" with me. We would pick wild flowers for our mothers along the road; we would run hand in hand, around all the trees in the yard, while giggling and acting goofy. We would ride the school bus for what seemed like hours, never growing tired of one another. Those were friends whom I never shared sorrow with, only happy innocent times of a beautiful childhood. I hope that all those children, wherever they are now, can still remember those happy simple times in which our faces would be tired from smiling so much by the end of the day.

As I grew into a teenager, there were more friends who came into my life. Going into high school, I still kept a lot of the friends that I had made at St. Mary's while attending first through eighth grade. My high school years led to slumber parties and record hops. There were always a lot of girls who would join in on the fun. Those were my "teenage friends." Those were the ones that I could talk to about anything, study together with, and share homework problems. Those were the ones who helped me through my first major boyfriend heartbreak, and would promise me that they would never let another guy hurt me. Those were the friends who would make homemade pizzas with me and we would stay up all night with each other. I don't even think they had frozen pizzas back then. If they did we never bought any.

I look back now and realize that those were the friends with whom I would cherish every high school memory. They were the ones who would help decorate for prom, go on double dates together, and stand hand in hand with me on the day of graduation as we cried our hearts out saying goodbye. We made promises that day of never losing contact with each other; but as the years passed suddenly; our promises were lost in time. A lot of them, too, have become a very special memory that I hold deep in my heart. Just thinking back on some of those fun times brings a smile to my heart now.

One instance that I will probably never forget about is a friend named Kathy, with whom I shared most of my high school years. In those days, kids weren't allowed to just take off and run all over. When we were about seventeen years old, her dad would allow her to put only so many miles on her car in one weekend. So we would meet our friend and classmate, Terry, uptown at the post office on Saturday nights. He would unhook her odometer on her car and then we would take off to ride around for hours or to go to the lake where they had dances. Then we would meet him back in town at 12:00 a.m., and he would hook it back up so her dad would not have any idea how many actual miles we had put on the car. We laugh now to think we actually pulled that back then, and got away with it. She did end up telling her parents when she got older. It was too late to get grounded by then.

As I married and started having children, again the friends would come and go. A classmate of mine from school whom I had never been close to at that time would then become my lifelong friend. I often thought it was strange that we never bonded going through twelve years of school together. Later in my life, I would come to realize that it was because God knew that I would need her so much more later on. Jane was the one who would share many a tear with me during my painful marriage. She would be there for me when I went through my divorce, and would be the one who would encourage me when I felt like I could not go on.

Even after she and her husband were stationed in Japan, we continued to keep in touch by writing monthly journals and mailing them at the end of every month so we would know what was going on with each other. It was in those journals that she would always remind me that God was there for me no matter what, and that it didn't matter what was going on, that He would give me the strength to endure. She encouraged me as I tried desperately to raise my children on my own after my divorce. It was she who brought me back to church in the only time that I had stayed away for a period of time.

In the year that I had quit going to church I wanted so much to "come back," but I was too stubborn. She would change my mind for me, which I would forever be thankful for. She was the one who gave me my "Let Go and let God" plaque which is still hanging in my bedroom today as a reminder that sometimes when we are overwhelmed with our trials and burdens, we need to turn them over to our Lord. She would become my "inspirational" friend. As we grow in our lives, our Heavenly Father has the wisdom to know which friends we need to be traveling with on this journey. Even though we are totally unaware of why someone comes into our lives at the time they do, God has already figured out His purpose for them. He sends them to us because He knows that we need them.

Jane and I are still close even though miles have kept us apart. Our hearts were always together. I know now that the reason we were not close in school was because God knew I would need her more as an "inspirational friend" later on in life. I ran across a poem recently that I had written for Jane many years ago. There was no title on it, but she knew the contents were all that mattered at the time.

God looked down upon me one day
And said "I think I need to find,
A very special friend for her
Someone that's one of a kind.

A very unique person
Who will help her through it all,
Someone whom she can depend on
And know she can always give a call.

A person whom she'll trust
An honest sort of friend,
Someone who'll always be there
Until the very end.

A certain guardian angel
To keep an eye on her,
Someone to wipe her tears at times
And have a shoulder to offer.

A person to help make her strong
At times she feels so weak,
A person to make her laugh
And put a smile upon her cheek.

Someone who may be far away
In distance, many miles,
But will keep a very close friendship
And help her through her trials."

God searched the whole world over
And kept busy that whole day long,
And then He sent that special someone
It was you all along.

I can't begin to thank Him enough
For sending you to me,
But I'll certainly ask Him to bless you
And to keep an eye on thee.

Another "inspirational friend" that God would send to me at a time in my life when I would need all the encouragement I could get was Jean. She was actually a cousin to me. I went to school with Jean's youngest son years ago, but I never really knew her that well. I knew her enough to know that she had not always had an easy life, and that her many trials had brought her very close to our Lord. She would be the friend that God sent me to always remind me of my mother's love after she died. There were lots of times during those years following mom's death, when I thought my broken heart would never feel whole again.

My daughter, Christie had just left for college, and my boys had just become teenagers. It was in those years that I would come to need the security of knowing that there was someone there who could calm me down when my tears would be falling like raindrops. Raising teenage boys after the death of their very special grandma was one of the most troublesome times I have ever been through.

God sent Jean to pray with me, to listen to me when I didn't know who else to confide in, and who would teach me five very important words that came to bring me strength in the days and months ahead. "Jesus, I trust in You." Those five little words proved to be the most powerful prayer I would ever learn. Sometimes I would call Jean crying, and ask her to pray for a particular situation. I felt in my heart the next day that God had heard her prayers because my heart would experience the peace that I thought I had lost. I would be stronger, and would be filled with a new ray of hope again. I still tease her about having an "800 # prayer line" to God. She gets so embarrassed, and says, "Oh Mary".

There is over a twenty-five year age difference in us, but when the Lord picks out your friends, age doesn't matter. It's the content of the heart and soul, and the substance of one's life experiences that can be shared with someone else to keep them going. Usually once a month, she has our Thursday night prayer group down to her house for cake and ice cream. We celebrate the birthdays that were shared that month. She always has the table set so beautifully, with a pretty tablecloth, and the burning candles give off a warm glow in her kitchen. A few flowers adorn the table, while soft music plays in the background. The presence of our Lord and His adorning Mother just fills the room. Jean, with a smile on her face says very softly, "Sit down everyone, and enjoy."

Whenever I walk into that kitchen, I can only imagine what it will be like when we go to meet our Creator. I picture it being the same way. God will meet us at the door, and His table will be set. His Son and our Blessed Mother will be right there with us. He will stand at the table and say to us, "Sit down everyone, and enjoy."

I can sense the angels sometimes in Jean's house, but when we get to see the Kingdom, they too, will greet us at the gates. I thank God for sending Jean to me at a time in my life when I really did need a lot of patience, and a lot of love and understanding. She has filled my heart with hope, and I know that I can carry her same words on to someone else someday that will need them.

I am so amazed sometimes at the timing of friends who show up in our lives. A few years after my mother had passed away, and my boys were choosing to take their own direction in their lives, which I knew was the wrong direction, I received a telephone call. I was asked if I would be interested in going to a weekly prayer group at our church on Thursday nights. Her name was Chris, and a friend of hers named Madonna were going to try and contact a few people to let them know. I told her that Thursday nights were my cleaning nights, and with ballgames, and other activities to attend with the boys still in school, I didn't know how often I would be able to attend, but I would probably come once in awhile. I went for the first one, and I knew then that this was to be my mission to bring my boys back to the Lord. Even the nights when I felt I was too tired to go, I still could hear God whispering to me that I would find peace there. I remember going one time, and I was crying so hard when I went that I sat in the back of our church so no one would see me. It didn't make any difference what was going on in my life when I went; I always felt a renewal of hope when I left. Chris and I began to bond in a way that I had never experienced with anyone. She had just gone through a lot with one of her teenage sons, and she knew exactly what I was going through, and what words I needed to hear. She felt my pain, she had cried my same tears, and she had walked that same exact journey that I was now traveling. Her heart had been touched with that same feeling of hopelessness, and there she was telling me that everything would be alright. She knew that it would be, because God was using her to remind me that there are always people out there who have carried that very same cross before, and they have survived. They have been through the trial, they have fallen but still gotten back up, they have cried a million tears, and they have prayed for strength and received it.

We went to our first Christ Renews His Parish retreat together, which drew us even closer into an intimate relationship of sharing God's love and His graces. Sometimes when I was really troubled, she would invite me down for coffee. We would get a cup and go sit on her couch with the candles lit, and ask God to send us His peace, and then we would sit quietly in the stillness of her living room, and pray a rosary together. I knew that God was listening. I felt His presence within my heart, and I knew that Chris and I had been joined at this time in our lives for a special reason. We could praise God together, we could thank Him for everything He had given to us, and yet we could pour out our hearts and souls to Him, asking Him to strengthen us, and to watch over our loved ones when they didn't know where they were sometimes going. This was the first time in my life that I had actually just sat down in someone else's home to quietly pray to our Heavenly Father. I knew then that God had blessed me with another "inspirational friend" that I would come to be so thankful for. I am overwhelmed sometimes at what God can do in our lives through someone else, and even at times when we don't even realize what He is doing.

God has blessed me throughout my entire life with the friends whom He knew I needed. I may not have always known why they had come into my life at the time they did, but I look back now and it all seems to fit so perfectly into a picture. These friends are the friends whom I hold dear in my heart. These are the friends who have shared my innermost happiness and my innermost sorrow. They are the ones, who have imprinted my heart with their gentleness and they have secured their loyalty within the deepest part of my being. Some of these friends were neighbors at one time, and have still remained close to me. Some have come into my life and then quietly left when God sent them on another journey. There have been life long friends, newly found friends, and some have already been called "home" by God. So many of them have changed my life, and each one of you knows who you are and how thankful I am to have shared the gift of your friendship.

I have been blessed by our Heavenly Father with friends as numerous and beautiful as a garden of flowers in the springtime. I don't even worry about who will be there for me in my future, because God has already taken care of that. He has lovingly been at work my entire life picking me flowers from His garden to send to me to brighten my life.

Friends are so important in this journey that we are traveling. Walking along hand in hand with someone makes any journey so much easier. Sometimes it's just so hard to believe when someone's hand fits yours so perfectly, but then God does plan everything perfectly, doesn't He?

ECCLESIASTES 4:10

"IF THE ONE FALLS, THE OTHER WILL LIFT UP HIS COMPANION. WOE TO THE SOLITARY MAN, FOR IF HE SHOULD FALL, HE HAS NO ONE TO LIFT HIM UP."

REFLECTION:

Everyone in his life needs close friends. Whom can you send a note to today to thank them for being there for you at all times?

Dear Heavenly Father

You know the day we are born whom You will be sending to us to be our friends. I thank You today, for all the precious freindships that have came into my life. Each one was sent for a special purpose, because You knew I needed them. Bless all those people who feel so alone, and uncared for. Send to them a treasured friendship that will always be there to hold their hand. Help me to always be a friend to all of Your children. In the most precious name of Your Son, Jesus Christ. Amen.

Time Is Precious

There are many sayings about "tomorrow." "I'll do it tomorrow," "I'll call her tomorrow," "tomorrow will be the first day of this or that." I think I have taken for granted my whole life that there will be a "tomorrow." The old saying is that we should live each day as if it were the last one. I have not lived my life according to that statement. Recently I was reminded of how precious time really is.

It's been nearly seven years ago since we moved into the house that my husband Victor and I are now living in. Right across the street from us were our neighbors, Marcia and Bob. Marcia had been in my mother and father's wedding nearly forty-eight years before that. I always thought it would be interesting to go visit Marcia and talk about my mother to find out what she was like when she was that young, and to maybe dicover things about her that I never knew myself. My mother had died four years before we moved in here, and I had plenty of time to think of things that I had never asked her.

Over the past nearly seven years, we have gotten together with Marcia and Bob on different occasions. They had us over for supper, or they'd come here for a quick bite on a few occasions. We'd meet uptown once in awhile and have supper together at our friendly little restaurant. We'd see them working in their yard, which was all the time in the summer, and we'd go over and stand and talk to them. If we needed to borrow anything, they'd tell us to come over and get it, and it was the same the other way around. They have been what you can call the "perfect neighbors." If they needed anything at all, we were here for them, and if we needed anything, they were there for us. I never really knew their children, because they were all younger then I in school. They had two girls and two boys, all of whom reached adulthood.

I learned a lot about them just by being neighbors. Every Sunday morning, I could almost always guess the time, by watching them pull out of their driveway to go to church. That was something they always did. I can hardly remember any time when they did not go. They depended on the Lord for all of their needs. They took the time on Sundays to go thank the Lord and offer up prayers of thanksgiving for everything they had. That to me has always said a lot about some one. When you see families who have gone through tragedies, and yet you can witness their unshaken faith, it helps us to truly understand the power of God.

Marcia and Bob had their faith tested over six years ago when their thirty-one year old son, Lonnie, was tragically killed in an accidental shooting. Instead of turning against God, they depended on Him for every ounce of strength that they needed to endure the loss. I'm sure at one time or another, when they sat within the silence of their own world, they might have questioned why it had to happen. If they did, no one ever knew it. The other man involved in the shooting lived around the corner and down the street from where they lived. He had to drive past Marcia and Bob's house everyday. It must have been hard for them to see him, but God gave them the courage they needed to be able to accept what they could not change. If there was ever any bitterness, they never showed it. They believed in God, and they depended on Him for the peace they needed to fill their hearts. Lonnie's death was sudden, no one had time to prepare for the loss that they were to experience, but they went on. They picked up their lives after the tragedy, placed them in our Loving Lord's care, and continued to walk on their journey in life.

A tragedy often brings about a time of realization. A time in which we step back to observe the realm of what time actually means. Often we change the ways in which we do things, and we try to make better use of our time. We realize that time is truly a precious gift from God, and it is so important to make every second of our lives count. It is so easy to make ourselves promises of things we will do, but our extremely busy lives sometimes keeps us from keeping those promises to ourselves.

As I said, for six and a half years, I had planned on walking across the street, and asking Marcia many questions about my mother. On Easter this year, I was standing at my kitchen sink, and I suddenly picked up the phone to call Marcia and Bob to see if they had any plans for lunch. I had thought of calling them on Saturday, but as always, I got too busy and did not get it done. I told them to just come over and eat with us about 1:00, if they didn't have plans. Shortly before 1:00, here they came across the yard. Some of our children made it home in time to eat, and some came later on in the day. My father came, and he really enjoyed visiting with Marcia and Bob. We had a wonderful and relaxing time, and really enjoyed being together.

It was great to share such a blessed holiday with such special friends. They stayed quite awhile and visited until everyone was starting to get the "after-eating yawns." As they stood at the door ready to leave, I hugged them both and thanked them for coming over and sharing Easter with us. As I hugged Marcia, I said, as I had said so many times before, "One of these days I'm going to come over and talk to you about mom."

As she had answered me many times before, she again replied, "You're welcome anytime," with a quiet and loving smile on her face.

As they left, my daughter Christie said to me, "How many more times are you going to say that?"

I replied with my regular answer, "Yes, I know, I really need to do that one of these days." "One of these days" I thought to myself. How often do we say that expression in regard to doing something that we can't make time for today? Little did I know that chilly Easter Sunday would be the last time I would ever have the chance to do what I had planned on doing for so long. That following Wednesday morning, Marcia had a massive stroke. She was taken by EMS to the local hospital twelve miles away, and then life flighted to a larger hospital forty five miles away. She went into a coma, went through surgery, but never came out of the coma. The following Thursday, eight days later, the angels came to take her home. During those eight days that she spent in a coma, her family and many, many friends were praying for a miracle.

The kind of miracle that we were all praying for was not the kind of miracle that God had planned. He had a miracle planned alright, a miracle of her being transformed from an earthly being into one of God's angelic spirits. He gave her a complete healing of body, mind and soul. During those long eight days as she lay in a coma in ICU, I had a lot of time to think. I had time to realize how precious time really is. Her husband and her children continued to stay by her side, trusting in God for whatever was about to happen. Bob's face showed worry and helplessness, but his words poured forth the faith that he had in God's plan. That Thursday night, as I was ready to walk out the door to go to my weekly Thursday night prayer group, I received the call. "Marcia passed away this afternoon about five o'clock."

I turned to my husband as I hung up the phone, tears running down my face, and I said, "Marcia is gone." At prayer group, all I could do was sob. My heart broke for her family whom I knew would miss her terribly. It also broke because I felt like God had nudged me so many times to go and have that conversation with her, and I never made it.

As we prayed, someone read about the joy between mother and son as they met once again in heaven, it was in reference to Mary meeting Jesus. To me, it was an affirmation that Marcia would be reunited with her son Lonnie. I also realized that someday she would see all of her family again, and she and Bob would never again be separated. The unending joy that she would be experiencing in this new life of hers would surpass any sad feelings we would have on earth over her death. God had just given to her another life, and now she would live with Him eternally in His Kingdom. Knowing how strong her faith was, reassured me that she would truly be met at the gates by our Loving Savior, and that she would forever live in His peace. I prayed for her family to be showered with strength and courage as they faced the days ahead.

I learned a very valuable lesson during that long week. I can say that I'll do something tomorrow, or that I'll start this or that tomorrow. But one thing I know for sure is that tomorrow may not be here. I can't go back now and have that conversation with Marcia, but I can make sure that the next time that I have such a strong feeling to do something, that I do it. I can listen quietly to God, and ask Him to take my hand and guide me to do what He wants me to do. I can tell other people to make a difference in people's lives today, just in case tomorrow doesn't come.

During that week, I approached a young man at work who is only twenty years old. I told him about the whole story. I shared with him that I knew it was God who was whispering to me to have that conversation, but whom I didn't listen too. I told him that life can seem really short sometimes, and we need to take every second and make it count. I don't know if he truly comprehended what I was trying to tell him. I know I never knew at that age how precious time was either. I know it now. I will share that with others and maybe it will save someone else the guilt of wishing they would have done something, and didn't do it.

As we stood in the back of the church on the day of her funeral, her loving husband stood by her casket, and shared Jesus' words with us on eternal life, and of the promises to all those who believe. He knew his wife was now with Jesus, because he had lived his life as a life of true faith, and he was aware of every promise that was ever given to him through the word of God. I know his heart must have been so sad, but I also know it must have been rejoicing for his wife, who would now have eternal life. I know that Marcia's family will miss her but I know their faith is strong. I've seen it before. God always gives the strength to people who need it. He never fails them.

I will miss seeing her out in the yard working with her beautiful flowers, and helping Bob to make a picture perfect looking postcard of their beautiful home and yard. What I will miss most is her beautiful heart and quiet smile. I will miss the opportunity that I thought I would always have to go talk to her. I pray that with this wisdom, I can help someone else who is traveling this faithful journey, to make good use of their time on earth. I pray that everytime we feel God pushing our shoulders a little to do something that we will react to it right away. God gave to us our lives, and we have no idea when He will be calling any of us home. If we treat each day as if it were our last, how much difference could we make in people's lives?

If you look up "time" in a dictionary, it will say something like this, "continuous period measured by clocks, watches, and calendars." I'd like to think of "time" as something being measured by love and laughter shared, good deeds being passed on, and an effort to make someone smile each day. To me, that is how I think God would want us to measure time.

I asked God to help me write a poem for Marcia's family that could help bring them comfort in their time of sorrow. She was such a beautiful woman, and I knew she deserved many wonderful words. Here are the words that He gave to me.

To Marcia, With Love

One spring day the angels came, to take God's child to His home above,
We weren't prepared for her to go, but He sent for her out of love.

Her faithfulness and love for Him, shone bright as His brilliant sun,
Her quiet smile and tenderness, she always shared with everyone.

She lived her life with thankfulness, for blessings God gave to her each day,
She shared His love with others, in a very quiet and special way.

With much love and dedication, she worked hard for her family and home,
She gave so much unselfishly, taking care of everything she owned.

She thanked God for every day, she wasn't one who wasted time,
She made every precious moment count, keeping everything in line.

So God looked down upon the earth, and said, "Marcia, my loving one,
I am now ready to reward you, your life on earth is now done.

It's time for you to come with Me, to My mansion in the sky,
I have so many gifts for you, don't be sad and please don't cry.

I promised you eternity, your new life has just begun,
You'll live with Me forever, this greatest victory you have won."

She caught a glimpse of Heaven, the beauty was beyond compare,
She said goodbye to us silently, as she left us unaware.

A choir of angels were singing, as she walked through Heaven's gate,
She knew her work on earth, made this splendor worth the wait.

She's now our guardian angel, watching over us day and night,
Heavenly blue skies and rainbows, are all within her sight.

Her memory will forever live on, being cherished deep within our hearts,
If we trust in God and pray to Him, someday we'll never again be apart.

If we listen very closely, we may hear her quietly say,
"Don't cry for me for now I'm free, my hand will reach for yours someday.

I'm now with my Heavenly Father, in His peaceful blue sky above,
Whenever you see my flowers bloom, remember me with love."

PSALM 39:6

"YOU HAVE GIVEN MY DAYS A SHORT SPAN; MY LIFE IS AS NOTHING BEFORE YOU."

REFLECTION:

None of us have any idea how long our journey will be on this earth. Is there someone who we need to talk too, in case one of our lives could be over soon?

Dear Heavenly Father

Sometimes it is so easy to assume that there will always be a tomorrow. Help us to realize just how precious time really is. Thank You for everyday that You allow us to celebrate. Remind us that each day as the sun rises, we need to say the things that people need to hear, visit friends whom we have neglected, and do the things that would be easier to put off another day. Help us to never have to regret that tomorrow never came. In the most precious name of Your Son, Jesus Christ. Amen.

A New Journey Traveled

Sometimes in life, we walk through wondering who we are, and why we are here. We wonder if we can ever make a difference in someone else's life. We can feel in our hearts that there is something missing in our own life, but no matter how hard we try, we can't find the answer. And then something happens that we are not expecting, and everything seems to fall into place. Have you ever experienced anything so powerful that you had to pinch yourself to see if it really happened? Well I did, and I'd like to share it with you.

Growing up in my parents' Christian home, and attending church my entire life, short of maybe a year, I truly believed that I had a close relationship with my Heavenly Father above. I knew the power of prayer, I always felt the need to pray, and I was never really too shy about sharing that feeling with others. I knew I depended on God for my every need, and I knew how I felt when I sat in His home thanking Him for everything I did have. So when I was invited to a Christ Renews His Parish weekend retreat at our neighboring parish at St. Michael's in 2001, I said "No, I don't think so!" After all, it was a weekend away after working all week. I had so many things to do, and people who needed me at home, people who depended on me for various things, that I absolutely could not commit myself to a retreat in which I would be gone all weekend. Looking back now, I can't even remember if I said "no" just one year, or if it was two years in a row. But when I finally said "Yes" to Sandy, who had been very persistent with me, I then started wondering why I had said yes. What could I gain from a church retreat when I already had a good relationship with the Lord? The more I started questioning things, the more curious I became. My good friend, Chris signed up to go, too. I was getting a little excited as the time got closer. Maybe nervous would be a better word than excited. That Saturday morning on the drive to Hicksville, only thirteen miles away, we wondered why we had ever said yes.

But the week before, my husband had come home from the men's retreat with a look in his eyes that I had never seen before. That thought kept coming to my mind on the trip over. He, too, had said "no" several times before finally agreeing to give up a weekend and go. Our priest Father Tom Oedy is absolutely loved and respected by everyone in our two parishes, so when he asked my husband after church one Saturday night about attending the retreat coming up, my husband couldn't say "no", and agreed to go.

When he had left for the retreat on that Saturday morning the week before, he, too, had left wondering why he was going, and wondering what it was going to be about. He was not at all excited about going away all weekend either. When he walked back in the house Sunday evening after the retreat, I knew that he was not the same person who had left there the morning before. Something in his eyes told me that something had happened. When I asked him how it had been, with tears in his eyes, all he could say was, "I saw the light and you're going to see it next weekend." That week seemed to bring that statement around many times, as I would jokingly say to him, "I'm going to see the light in a few more days." And now my friend and I were on our way.

When Chris and I arrived, and signed in, we realized we were not going to be sitting together. I am not shy, but yet I could feel a little apprehension about being with a lot of women whom I did not know. One thing we all had in common was the fact that no one really knew why we were there. It was so obvious that we had all gone because we had felt the need to for some reason. I didn't know at that time that God had already chosen us for this weekend, because He knew the reasons we all needed to be there. It truly was a weekend of sharing God's love, peace and forgiveness. It was a weekend of walls coming down, hearts opening up, and new relationships forming through the glory of God. I experienced things that I had never felt before. There was a "spiritual director" leading the weekend and her name was

Carol. I heard prayers come from her lips that I knew came straight from the Lord. I knew they were messages meant for every one of us to hear. I heard stories of how God had worked in people's lives in ways I never thought were possible. I found out that the relationship that I had with God was not nearly as deep and intimate as I thought it was. I learned more about myself, I learned more about God, and I learned that I have never walked this journey by myself and that I never would.

I realized in one short weekend that God had never left my side for one second of my life, and that I could count on Him to be there with every step of my future. I learned that the bitterness and hatred that I had been carrying around in my heart for years toward my ex husband had suddenly been lifted off my heart. That same place deep within my being was now filled with a peace that I could not understand. I felt the feelings of despair that I had when wondering if my boys would come back to the faith, suddenly turn into feelings of hope and encouragement. When I left there that Sunday evening, I knew without a doubt that "With God all things are possible." I had seen Him at work in a way I had never seen before. I had felt the presence of the Holy Spirit like nothing I ever imagined. I was at a loss for words. I had truly "saw the light," and I now knew what the look was in my husband's eyes the week before. It was the look of amazement to actually witness the extreme power of God at work in so many lives in one weekend. It was a modern day miracle that I had been called to be a part of. Looking back, I wouldn't have missed it for the world. And all along, I had wondered what I could gain from this weekend with God. I had no idea what He had in store for me, but I did know that I had been on a roller coaster ride for two days, I just didn't know at the time that the ride had only just begun. All the way home, Chris and I could not stop talking about what we had witnessed. We were spiritually flying so high that I felt it would never end.

Later that evening as I sat down at my kitchen table to try and sort out all that I had consumed that weekend, my mind raced excitedly. It was time to grab a pen because I was bursting with words to explain all that I had seen and felt. God helped me put those feelings into this poem.

A Spiritual Uplift

Christ Renews His Parish
Is a weekend for all to attend,
It will really lift your spirits
And help broken hearts to mend.

The presence of the Holy Spirit
Will surround you everywhere,
You'll meet loving and caring people
And make new friends who really care.

It will give you hope if you are down
And put laughter into your heart,
It will bring God back into your life
If you felt you were drifting apart.

Your heart and soul will feel a peace
Like they've never felt before,
Guilt, despair, and bitterness
Will be gone forevermore.

The sun will be shining brighter
And your clouds will drift away,
Your heart will be filled with so much hope
That you'll look forward to the next day.

You'll be thankful for all the little things
That never crossed your mind,
And the rainbow you've been looking for
Might just be easier to find.

You'll share joy and tears and laughter
And hugs will be everywhere,
You'll find someone who has shared your pain
And you will feel blessed that you are there.

God's presence will be everywhere
As He watches from His sky above,
Your spirit will be overflowing
With joy and peace and love.

I had no idea what God had planned for me in the next three years that would follow that retreat. If I had, I probably would have run and hid. But the joy and contentment that filled my heart in the days to come certainly overpowered any insecurity my heart held at the time.

I was now on a new journey, and I was going to be traveling to places that I had never been before. I was on a path that led to the deepest part of my soul, a path that I had never taken. A path that I never even knew existed. I was now walking in God's world, and my heart trembled every time I realized what was happening. I soon told many others of my excitement in hopes that everyone I loved would someday be able to experience this same incredible feeling.

I joined the Christ Renews His Parish team two weeks after attending that retreat. I was so anxious to be a part of the energy that I had felt during those two days. I wanted to be one of those "sisters in Christ" that had been bonded by God in a way I had never felt before. I yearned to have a closer friendship with God, and I knew that I would be able to find it through this team of disciples whom God had chosen to do His work. I had never been so excited in my life to "go to work," as I was in joining this team which was working all for the glory of their Savior. That night of discipleship, when we were given the opportunity to join the team, I heard the words "You're going to save a soul." clearly in my mind. Not realizing what I was really hearing, I questioned it "What?", and sure enough there it was again "You're going to save a soul." I had never in my life heard words so clearly and loudly in my head as I did that night. Tears came upon me as if there was no control. "What did this mean?" "What was happening to me?" I did not know the answers to any of these questions, but one thing I was sure of was that I did want to be a part of whatever God was planning for me. Later I would find out that His plan for me was already in progress, and the very next year I would be standing before sixty women sharing my life and telling how God had held my hand through every step.

In the year leading up to that witness, I grew so much in my faith. I had really thought that I was doing O.K., but working for my Lord made me realize how lazy I had been in so many areas of my life. I used to sit at the railroad tracks to wait on a train, and grumble the whole time because I was in a hurry. Now I would quietly sit there and say Our Father's, and Hail Mary's, for someone who needed prayers. It wasn't necessarily someone I knew, but I would just pray for anyone who could be in trouble at that time, whether it be a pregnant teenager, a drug addict, someone who had just lost someone they loved. I found that there was always someone who needed help, and if I could lift someone up in prayer, then that made me feel like I was really making a difference. Even if I never found out who the prayers were for, I knew someone was going to benefit from them. I found out that year that from the time I left my factory to go home and eat lunch, I could say exactly ten Hail Mary's. It felt so much better praying then complaining to myself because I was having a rotten day. So many things in my life changed that year and with my husband being on the men's team, we grew together spiritually. There was more to a marriage then just sitting beside each other in church each week. I was so happy and content with having found someone that I could share my faith with, that I did't even know there was so much more awaiting in our relationship.

When the weekend came for "our retreat" that we had worked on all year, I was so nervous. I knew that God would be helping us make it a success, but I was also praying that I would be able to feel His presence as I gave my witness. It was so much more than I had ever imagined. I felt like He was standing right behind me with His hands on my shoulders. There was a part of my life that had been very painful and had held a lot of bad memories and bitter feelings. God used that witness to bring about a miraculous healing within myself, and to give me a friendship with someone with whom I never thought that our relationship could ever be healed. God used His forgiveness to show me what I needed to do in my own life. He used me to share that with others who needed it as much as I did. That year again, I felt like I could not get any higher.

I joined team again, after that weekend, for the following year. That year I was discerned to be the liturgist, which meant I would provide the music for all the meetings, and be in charge of the music for the retreat the next year. I was not at all happy when I realized what God had planned for me. After all, I was not musically inclined by any means, and I never sang in the choir or played any instruments. My friend Chris had been the liturgist that year before. She is a beautiful singer, she plays organ for our church, and also plays guitar. She did a beautiful job using her God given musical ability at the retreat, and "I" was going to have to follow in her footsteps. No matter how hard I tried to say "no" to the Lord, someone else would affirm me for that position. I felt like a fool arguing, but I just couldn't think that this was what the Lord really wanted me to do. Well, I lost, and I was discerned for liturgist.

That year God showed me that when He wants you to do something, He provides everything you need to do a good job for Him. The year before that, I had bought a lot of relaxation C.D.'s and some Christian CD's at a garage sale. Those ended up being used at the meetings throughout that next year. The Lord had me picking out music the year "before" I was even discerned to be liturgist. How could I ever doubt what He was doing in my life? Each meeting I would wait till the last minute and then rush around to find a song to play at the beginning. It never failed, I would open up my disorganized cupboard only to have a CD fall out, and for some reason I would look at it and know which one was supposed to be played. Then at the meeting, I would find out that one of the girls was going through something, and desperately needed to hear the words of that song. God never let me down that whole year, He did all the work. All I had to do was follow Him and listen when He spoke.

Our spiritual director Vicki found out that summer that she had cancer. We were all devastated when we heard the news. We had no idea that God would use this incident to deepen our faith and to give witness to the power of sisters in Christ praying for one another. She had to go through chemo and eventually lost her hair. The first meeting after that, all of us "sisters" came wearing baseball caps to give her support and to show her that we were all in this together, and that we would walk with her every step. God's healing hand was upon her that year, as she survived, and we all watched her faith grow in multitudes, along with the rest of us.

A few weeks before the retreat that next year, I had a horrible day at my factory job. Our team had a night of reconciliation, and I was not even in the mood to go. A friend of mine at work had talked about her mother and all the talks they had. I went back to my table after break and the tears just started falling because I missed my own mother so much. I felt cheated that I was only forty years old when my mother had passed away ten years before that. So when I walked into our meeting that night and saw "Mommy Pat," as I called her, I missed my mother even more. Pat had been at the retreat where I had given my witness, and for some reason, we bonded right away. She reminded me a lot of my own mother, for she was petite and short with brown hair. There was something very special about her.

During reconciliation, I shared my feelings with Father Tom about me being mad about not having my mother around, and how some women who I knew were a lot older then I still had their mothers and grandmothers. I remember crying and telling him that the reason I missed my mom so much was because whenever something was wrong in my life, all she had to do was put her arms around me, pat my back and say to me, "Everything's going to be alright, Mary, I love you." I told him I needed to hear that so bad at times, and now I couldn't. Before I was ready to take my candle to the altar, he said he needed to talk to me about something. He asked me if I would consider being the spiritual director for the team that next year. He said he felt that God was calling me to do it. I just started crying. I told him I didn't know, that I was not an organized person and I couldn't see me being capable of doing something like that. I told him I would think about it and let him know. He told me not to think about it but to pray about it instead.

As I was carrying my little red candle up to the altar, all I could think about was how tough it is for me to make decisions. I pictured myself infront of my refrigerator on my lunch time trying to decide which kind of yogurt I wanted to eat. I thought to myself, "How can I ever make a decision this huge?" I sat my candle down, genuflected, and told God that I was going to need a lot of help in making this decision. I turned and walked down the side aisle, stopping to give a few girls a hug. And then I saw her. "Mommy Pat" was sitting by herself at the end of the aisle. Our eyes met, and as I leaned over to hug her, we embraced tightly as she patted my back and said, "Everything's going to be alright, Mary, I love you." Tears came rolling down my face as we held each other tight. She had no idea what had just happened, and I wasn't sure if I did either. It was something I could not explain, and the moment was one which I will remember as long as I live. I stopped hugging her long enough to pull away from her and look at her face, because I really was believing I would see my mother's face as I looked into her eyes. She would not find out for weeks later that God had used her to answer a huge prayer of mine. She did not know her words were truly my mother's words, and that she made everything that night, and in the year to come, "alright". I knew in that moment that God wanted me to be His spiritual director that year, and I knew that all my insecurities and fears would be overpowered by God's love and the ability that He would give to me to do His work, only because I answered "Yes" when I heard Him call.

I don't know if Pat understood why any of that happened. When I ask her why she said those words to me, she had no answer. She said that they just came out. God knew exactly the right words that I needed to hear at the time, and He knew the right person who needed to say them to me. "Mommy Pat," of all people, was the one who reminded me of my mother since the day we had met. Now she was saying my mother's words to me at a time when I needed it the most. Experiencing this profound situation helped me to understand exactly how things work out at times. I was amazed at what God had done and I was grateful for being a part of it. I was astonished at how He works and how quickly prayers can be answered at times. I was even more amazed at the things I was being allowed to witness. I was being blessed in a way I never had before, and my heart was so full of gratitude that it was overflowing.

A few weeks after that all happened, we had our next retreat. This was the weekend that I would be the liturgist. God took care of every intricate detail that I had fretted about. The weekend was another God-filled experience that just was overwhelming to sit back and watch. People came, as I did my first year, not knowing why and some not really wanting to be there. They left feeling the presence of God working in their lives as never before. I wondered to myself how this could keep happening year after year. I came to the conclusion that when God is making something happen, and He is choosing people to experience it, that you can expect anything to happen. It was another beautiful weekend that kept me flying for weeks.

Being called to be spiritual director gave me another year on the team. I was looking forward to it, although I was absolutely terrified. I often would have my doubts about my capabilities, wondering how I could ever "spiritually direct" twenty women, but everytime I found myself questioning God's purpose in my life, something would happen that would literally chase those fears away. As I said before, if God chooses you to be His disciple, then He will give you all the tools you need to do His work. He will not set you out to build a house without a hammer and nails in your hand. He will not give you a spiritual job to do without giving you the prayers and the encouragement you need to succeed. He will always provide what you need and at the right time.

There is a "lay director" that works with the "spiritual director" all year long. God discerns someone for that, too. I, being human as I am, worried about that also. "What if someone gets chosen and we don't work well together?" "What if we don't agree on everything that needs agreed upon?" The "what if's" stayed in my mind no matter how much I prayed about it. Then came the day of discernment, and I found out that He had chosen "Diane" for the position. She had attended the same first retreat that I had. In fact, the reason we became so close was because we took our smoking breaks outside in the cold together. She, too, had joined team that first year that I had, and we had grown very close in those two years together. And now God had chosen her to be my "right hand woman" as we grew together with this new team that He was forming for the next retreat.

We often laughed knowing that when we were standing in the cold two years before, not knowing each other at all, that we were going to be joined as "sisters in Christ" someday, and that God already knew why all of this was happening. He already had both of us picked out at the time to be doing this work for Him.

That year on team proved the same things over and over again. God gave us all the tools we needed to do His work. He gave us the encouragement we needed when we felt helpless. He gave us the words we needed when someone needed His help in something. He gave us the wisdom that we thought we didn't have in the beginning to guide the team on this journey, and He gave us His sunshine to light our path when things got dark. That year when Diane and I worked together, sometimes we would have phone bills with seven hundred some minutes' long distance on them. Our husbands would tease us because we only lived fifteen miles apart, and we could have driven to each others' houses for nearly free compared to the phone bills. She and I were truly blessed by God to have been given the friendship we shared and the bonding that we needed in order to do His work.

In October of that year, 2003, is when my dear Aunt Helen got sick and went home with the Lord. She died at 1:30 a.m. on a Sunday morning, and our team had a meeting that Sunday afternoon at 2:00. I debated about going, but I knew I needed to be with my sisters in Christ. I also knew that I would be able to gain strength from them, and that God would shower His words among them, so that I would be comforted at this time of sorrow. It all happened just as I knew it would. Our meeting was even scheduled to be in the church that day, which was unusual. As I sat among my sisters, tears fell easily as I wondered what I would ever do without my Aunt Helen, but as I looked around, I knew that God had given me this team to help me through this time. I knew in my heart, that as always before, He would give me the strength I needed and the people in my life with whom I could depend on for support.

Our retreat was three months later in January. I kept wondering how this one would be, since Diane and I would be sitting at a table with Father Tom instead of mixing in with the rest of the participants. Again, I experienced things unfelt before. Diane and I actually were given a power surge by the Holy Spirit; the gift of laughter which I thought for a few minutes might not ever end. We even had to quietly leave the room long enough to compose ourselves. I don't think I have ever laughed that hard in my life, but I hope I do again someday.

It was incredible to watch everything going on in that room, knowing that the true presence of God was everywhere. He touched each heart in that room, and we knew by watching them that their lives were changed forever, as ours had been only three years before that. Another year, another incredible weekend of seeing the hand of our Heavenly Father at work, and another blessing of being able to be a part of it. The whole team did a wonderful job, and those who were so nervous about their roles found out that God gave them everything they needed.

One of the witnessers was actually touched so much by the Holy Spirit that our whole team was shocked when she got up and started talking. She was the shy one, who was terrified to get up infront of anyone, let alone sixty women, but once the Holy Spirit took over she stepped out of her shell and spoke like we had never heard her before. There wasn't a shy bone in her body at that moment. Our team looked around at one another with smiles on our faces and thumbs up. We sat and watched as we realized the power of God. We were amazed at what we were seeing. To this day, I don't think she realizes what happened up there.

As the retreat came to an end, I could feel my heart being torn because I knew that my time on this journey was coming to an end. My favorite expression that year when someone was troubled became, "It'll all come out in the wash." They knew that it meant, "Quit worrying about everything, because God will take care of all of it the way He has planned, so why worry at all?"

Diane and I stood outside in the cold after the retreat was over that night, thanking God for bringing us together in the beginning, and for letting us share so much together in that year. He had bonded us so close that one of us would start a sentence and the other one would finish it. We stood in the cold wondering if we would remain as close as we were then. We should have known that when God brings two people together for His honor that nothing will be able to separate that relationship. We cried until the freezing air almost turned our tears into miniature icicles. We laughed until our stomachs hurt so bad that we were holding them. We hugged like we would never be given the chance again. And when we left, our hearts knew that we had been given the chance to grow together in God's love in a way that neither of us had ever experienced before. We had been blessed in a way that was not even able to be explained in any words. But most of all, we left knowing that all of this had happened, because we both had taken a chance and said "yes" to God. Through all of the insecurities and fears, God had held our hands every step of the journey, a journey I had never traveled before, but one in which I learned so much about my faith and the faith of others. A journey in which I hoped I would forever stay on, and never lose my step or direction.

"Deb" went on to be the next spiritual director. In that following year she doubted herself many times, just like I had the year before. But I heard that she done a fantastic job leading the women on team. God worked in her life in so many ways, and she gave Him all the glory.

One night, weeks after Diane and I had stood in that parking lot freezing, I was remembering all that I had experienced while working for the Lord on that team. I remembered the first night of discipleship when I heard those words, "You're going to save a soul." I looked back into my memory and realized that the next year after that first retreat was when I started visiting my uncle again, whom I had neglected over the years of working and raising a family. He was now old and fragile, and not ornery like I had remembered him growing up. He was in a nursing home, and I think he knew that his days on this earth were numbered.

It was then that God had given me the courage to ask my uncle if I could pray with him. I didn't remember him or my aunt ever going to church at all, and I don't remember them ever talking about faith, or their feelings about a relationship with God. But I knew at that time, God was calling me to talk to my uncle about His love and forgiveness. It was then that I would hold my dying uncle's hands in mine, and pray that God would bring him peace and forgiveness in his life. In those moments it didn't matter whether he had ever had a relationship with God. Now he was being given the chance to tell God he wanted Him as his personal Lord and Savior.

Do I know if that was the voice in my heart, that night of discipleship, trying to tell me of this situation to come? I may never know. Was it my uncle whose soul I might have helped save without even being aware of it? I don't know the answer to any of these questions, but what I do know is that God had given me the tools again to do His work. I had been given courage to step forward and ask someone if I could pray with them, not even knowing how they felt about prayer. I was given the right words through the power of the Holy Spirit when I prayed, because when I would finish, not knowing anything that I had really said, my uncle cried and smiled at me as if I had just handed him a million dollars. He looked into my eyes and said, "Thank You, Mary." I left the nursing home crying also. I would look up into the sky saying, "Thank You, God." My uncle died soon after that. At his graveside, I shared with the rest of the cousins whom I had not seen in years the wonderful and precious moments that my uncle and I had shared in the final year of his life.

The first retreat, the yearning of wanting to make a difference in someone's life, was now fulfilled. I had learned, I had gained, and I had shared with as many of God's children as I could what happens when your heart is open to all that He has to offer you. I became almost obsessed with bringing more people to God. I became so uplifted and energized when I was doing His work. I fell in love with God all over again, in the most intimate kind of relationship that I could have.

Now that part of the journey was over, and I would find another path to walk on and other means of sharing God's love and joy with others. After I went off team last year, later on in the year was when my father passed away. But the love and support that I gained from working with God's chosen disciples in the years before that would give me the courage I needed to say goodbye to him.

It's been said for many years that God works in mysterious ways, and I believe that without a doubt. He always knows what we need, whom we need in our lives, and the things we need to keep going. He always gives us the tools we need. In the witness that I gave the year I was spiritual director, I asked the Lord to help me find the words that explained how I felt. The witness I gave was "New Life In Christ."

A New Life In Christ

I have a new life in Christ, He now lives deep within my heart,
My life has changed, I'm not the same, I've been given a brand new start.

His presence was always with me, He guided me each and everyday,
But somehow it is different now, I love Him in a whole new way.

The trials and tribulations in my life, He helped me to get through,
But now He's in every breath I take, and in everything I do.

This new life in Christ has really changed, my entire heart and soul,
This joyous feeling inside of me, will praise Him forever more.

I used to see His presence, in the beauty of the trees,
But now I feel His presence, burning deep inside of me.

My tears used to fall like raindrops, when hard times would come my way,
But now my tears can easily fall, from the joy He sends each day.

The struggles really never end, and challenges come and go,
The only difference now is that, His hope lives within my soul.

I used to share with family and friends, of His faithfulness from above,
Now my need is to tell the whole world, of His forgiveness and glorious love.

When I see Christ hanging on the cross, and I know He died just for me,
I now feel the guilt inside my being, and I cry with humility.

So many things are different now, than what they ever were before,
My Lord and Savior lives in me, I'll be His servant forever more.

My life has changed and I have grown, My spirit has been set free,
I am a different person now, I have a new life in Christ, you see.

That first retreat that I went too, not really even wanting to go, changed everything in my life. I wonder how different my life might have been if I could have experienced something like that when I was younger. But I am so thankful I had the opportunity now that I will always thank God for inviting me when I didn't even think I needed it.

Our parish has been so blessed with the presence of our Father Tom. Because of him, we have been given the chance to feel the presence of the Holy Spirit at these retreats. He has taught us so much about what God can do in our lives. Having him to talk to is probably like it was when Christ walked this earth. He seems to have such a close relationship with our Heavenly Father, and He seems to always have the right things to say when we are lost. He knows what it is to serve the Lord, and he puts a yearning in our hearts to do the same. I have been blessed to have been a part of the Christ Renews His Parish team. I have been blessed by being in a parish where I have truly experienced the love of God through the teachings of a remarkable and loving priest who has guided us into this new journey.

Sometimes we seem to just drift along through life, not realizing anything that God is trying to tell us. And then spring comes about, buds turn into beautiful flowers, cocoons turn into beautiful butterflies, and lives blossom into the lives that God had intended us to have. If we open our hearts to Him, and we listen when He speaks, we will be able to clearly see the meaning of our lives.

Being a servant to God is the most gratifying job I have ever done. I used to get up in the morning and have my day planned. Now when I awake I ask the Lord what He would like me to do today. It is so exciting to see what happens sometimes, and to see the people that He sends to you that either need you or you need them. He is a God of knowledge and wisdom, love and compassion. If we can only turn our lives into the lives that He planned for us, we will be much happier in everything that we do. Try it for a day, and see what happens, you might be amazed. You might find out that you have gifts that He has given you that you weren't even aware of. As I said earlier, He always gives us what we need to do His work. It is up to us to open our hearts and listen to what He asks of us. He asked me to go to that first retreat, and I am so thankful that I said "yes." Don't be afraid of what He might be asking of you. He may be trying to open a whole new door for you that you never imagined. He may just have something very exciting waiting for you behind that door.

It's very seldom that we go through a birthday or a Christmas and not open any of the presents we received. We are usually excited just anticipating what might be inside, and the one who gave them to us is usually just as excited as we are to see the expressions on our faces when we open them. Yet God gives us so many gifts throughout our lives, and sometimes we never open them. Can you imagine how you would feel watching someone you gave something too, and yet they never opened it? God is watching and waiting patiently for us to receive and acknowledge the gifts that He has given to us. Sometimes those gifts that we were not aware of, may just be the "tools" we need to take the new journey that we have never traveled.

A Burning Flame

If each of us lights a candle
For all of the world to see,
Our love will spread throughout the earth
We will bring peace and harmony.

If we share God's love with just one friend
And let them know He's always there,
Then maybe they will turn to God
And bow their head in prayer.

We can bring hope to all the world
If we stand united as one,
If we share a candle with just one friend
Our mission has now begun.

A candle burning in just one heart
Can wipe someone's tears away,
It can help their clouds start to fade
Making way for a sunny day.

It will help their heart to heal
If their heart was broken in two,
It will help them to truly believe
That hope lives in me and you.

They will see a star more clearly
That shines bright in the sky above,
They will feel God's love surround them
As He sends them His blessing of love.

A burning flame in a heart and soul
Can help miracles start to begin,
If we can pass just one flame on
A lost soul we might just win.

So let us stand hand in hand
As we light our candles one by one,
And maybe someday this world will shine
As bright as God's miraculous sun.

I wrote this poem the first year on the Christ Renews His Parish team to go along with the theme of sharing Christ's light with others.

Father's Loving Care

I pause to look back upon my life
As I recall its ups and downs,
I thank my heavenly Father today
For always being around.

He stood by me when times were sad
And He helped my tears to end,
He gave me sunshine on the cloudy days
He helped my broken heart to mend.

There were times when I would drift away
And forget that He was there,
There were times I'd forget to thank Him
For all of His tender loving care.

Somehow it didn't matter to Him
For He knew that I loved Him still,
Even when I'd argue with Him
Wanting things my way instead of His will.

I owe Him for each breath I take
And for the gifts He's given to me,
I never would have made it on my own
If He hadn't always guided me.

When I laugh, I know He'll smile with me
And when I fall, He'll always be there,
No fear will ever come to me
I'm wrapped in my Father's loving care.

This poem I also wrote that first year of being on team. I gave a witness that year on "Father's Loving Care", and I ended my witness with this poem.

Please Give Me Your Hand

Please give me your hand, and let me be your friend,
Let me try to hold you up, when you feel like it's the end.

Let me offer you my shoulder, if you ever need to cry,
I won't need an explanation, you don't have to tell me why.

I always want to be there, when your skies are dark and gray,
I want you to depend on me, with each new rising day.

Whenever your heart is burdened, and you don't know what to do,
I will offer you encouragement, to help put a smile on you.

Please give me your hand, and let me be your friend.....

When your tears are falling like raindrops, and you think they'll never end,
I'll say an extra prayer for you, to help your heart to mend.

If your burdens seem so heavy, that you feel you can't go on,
Just remember that tomorrow, brings a brand new hopeful dawn.

When you're holding on to hope, but it seems to be slipping away,
Just try and always remember, I'm only a prayer away.

Whenever you're tired and lonely, and you see no end in sight,
I'll always be here to remind you, you must never give up the fight.

Please give me your hand, and let me be your friend.....

If the journey that you're traveling, looks like miles and miles ahead,
Just take a few small steps, and gaze at the shining sun instead.

If you wake up in the morning, and your heart feels sad and blue,
Just remember someone is out there, praying quietly for you.

And when you feel like no one cares, just look at the peaceful sky,
Pray that your heart can feel that peace, as each day passes by.

Whenever you see the rainbow, after the storm has gone away,
Remember that it's a promise, that someone's always guiding your way.

Please give me your hand, and let me be your friend…..

When you see the majestic sunset, setting in the tranquil sky so blue,
I want you to look for the miracle, there may be one hidden just for you.

When you see the mysterious full moon, shining forth its' brilliant light,
Remember there's hope in tomorrow, someone
will guide you through the night.

When the rain keeps falling endlessly, think of all the strength you need,
Call on the ONE who can give all things,
while you pray on bended knee.

Someday, you may hear a voice in the wind, saying quietly, "I love you,
Please give me your hand, let me be your friend,
I will always be here for you."

This poem was written the second year on team when Vicki had cancer. She continued to remind us of God's faithfulness even through her trials. She told us that He never let go of her hand the whole year. That became our theme for the retreat-To tell others to never let go of His hand and to always hold on to each other's hands.

I Can Only Imagine

I can only imagine, what it will be like,
To stand at Heaven's gate, before our Heavenly Father's sight.

Have our hearts ever experienced, the peace that we will feel?
Will we be completely breathless, will we even know it's real?

Will our souls be pure and beautiful, as the freshly fallen snow?
Will the stars glitter like diamonds, leaving the sky all aglow?

Will the sun shine forever, even brighter than it does here?
Will there be beautiful lakes, which are really crystal clear?

I can only imagine, what it will be like.....

Will there be colored rainbows, adorning the entire sky?
Will we know within our heart, that we will never again cry?

Will it feel as fresh and cleansing, as a gentle rain in the spring?
Will we be forever smiling, as the angels start to sing?

Will we hear God whispering, "My precious child, welcome home!"
Will we even be aware, that we will never again be alone?

Will we feel the same warmth, as the gentle breeze in the fall?
Will we be forever thankful, God has finally made His call?

I can only imagine, what it will be like.....

Will the excitement in our hearts, be burning way deep down inside?
Will our shame be washed away, never feeling the need to hide?

Will all the sadness in our lives, be gone forevermore?
Will we be thankful for the trials, that helped us learn to soar?

Will our questions all be answered, that we asked while here on earth?
Will we be able to clearly see, our entire journey since our birth?

Will our loved ones all be waiting, to meet us at the gate?
Will the love within our hearts, tell us the time was worth the wait?

I can only imagine, what it will be like.....

Will there be someone standing there, that we felt we never knew?
Will they tell us that we touched them, and that their life was made brand new?

Will we kneel before Our Lord, as He wipes our tears away?
Will He wrap His arms around us, as we thank Him for this day?

Will He somehow find us worthy, to walk His streets of gold?
Will He tell us that we listened and we did the things He told?

Will He take us by the hand, and walk forever in His light?
What will it really be like, when we stand before His sight?

I CAN ONLY IMAGINE, WHAT IT WILL BE LIKE....

This poem was written the year I was spiritual director for the team. This was the year that my dear Aunt Helen passed away in the fall, and the retreat was that coming winter. I often tried to imagine what it was like for her when she finally made it home. That became our theme for the retreat.

I'll Praise You With Glory

I come before Your presence Lord, how can You find me worthy,
I come here stained with sin and pride, but yet You still do love me.

You shed Your blood and died for me, You hung upon that cross,
You did it all for me, my Lord, You knew that I was lost.

I've tried so hard to walk with You, but I've stumbled many times,
You took my hand and pulled me up, forgiving me each and every time.

I stand before You meek and small, my heart is open to You,
Please bless me with Your presence Lord, in everything that I do.

Your love for me is always there, You've never let me down,
You've filled my life with so much hope, when no one else was around.

You wiped my cheeks when tears did fall, You filled my heart with love,
You gave me more than I deserved, as You watched me from above.

I want to love You so much more, than I have ever known,
I want to make You proud of me, till the day You call me home.

I wonder if I'm strong enough, to follow You each day,
You've promised You would stay with me, and guide me along the way.

I know as long as You are there, the sun will always shine,
The rainbow in the sky tells me, You're with me all the time.

I want to live my life for You, so that when my days are done,
You'll gently reach as I come to You, saying I've been a faithful one.

I can't imagine doing anything, that would keep me away from You,
You've blessed my life in so many ways, I want to sing a song for You.

My heart is filled with thankfulness, for the life You've given to me,

I want to share Your faithfulness, with everyone I see.

And someday when my work is done, and my spirit has been set free,
We'll meet in Your glorious home above, will I be worthy, Your Majesty?

I love You Lord with all of my heart, consume me with Your love,
I'll praise You with glory each day of my life, till I can be with You above.

The Lord gave me the words to this poem the year after I went off team. I had been talking to Jodi, the team's new lay director, and she told me their theme was to give praise and honor to His name.

I PETER 4:10-11

"AS EACH ONE HAS RECEIVED A GIFT, USE IT TO SERVE ONE ANOTHER AS GOOD STEWARDS OF GOD'S VARIED GRACE. WHOEVER PREACHES, LET IT BE WITH THE WORDS OF GOD; WHOEVER SERVES, LET IT BE WITH THE STRENGTH THAT GOD SUPPLIES, SO THAT IN ALL THINGS, GOD MAY BE GLORIFIED THROUGH JESUS CHRIST, TO WHOM BELONG GLORY AND DOMINION FOREVER, AMEN."

RELECTION:

God has given each one of us very unique and special gifts, designed just for us. Have you unwrapped God's gifts to you and are you using them to glorify His name?

Dear Heavenly Father

You have planned our lives from the beginning of our days. You have given us meaning to our lives, and have sent us here on a journey to do Your will. Help us to feel the excitement when we do things to please You. It is so easy for us to believe that we are already where we should be spiritually. Please give us the wisdom we need to do Your will, and the courage we need to feel capable of whatever You have planned for us. Thank You for all of our gifts, for our bothers and sisters in Christ, and for trusting us enough to serve You. In the most precious name of Your Son, Jesus Christ. Amen.

My Mothers' Love

The wind blows restlessly today as the sun fights so hard to stay shining in the gray casted sky. It is Mothers' Day, and my mind is as restless as the wind outside. I see the branches blowing fiercely, and I wonder when they will calm down and become peaceful again. I wonder too, when my mind will do the same.

Mothers' Day brings to me a mixture of so many feelings that it's sometimes hard to sort them all out. Unlike most people, God blessed me with two mothers. One that would find out that she was carrying the gift of life inside of her, and have to make a decision of what she should do in her situation, and one that would raise me as her very own daughter. I have been so blessed since the beginning.

Today I can't help but think of my biological mother, wondering what she thought when she found out about her pregnancy with me. What were the circumstances that led to that day? Did she have support or did she go through nine months of carrying me by herself? I try to place myself in her situation, and it's so hard for me to do. I can't help but love her, even if I don't know her, because I can't help but somehow feel the pain that must have burdened her heart all that time. You see, I was inside of her, and although I was a mere seed growing into this life, I was still connected to her from the beginning. She carried me for nine months and gave birth to me. I wonder now if she gazed into my eyes, with pain in hers, knowing she would not be able to give me what she knew I would need.

I sometimes wonder in those five months before she signed the papers how often she saw me, and how she felt when she held me in her arms. Did her heart break in a million pieces, or did she feel contentment in her heart knowing she was making the right decision? Did she cry as she said goodbye to me? Did she kiss me on the forehead as she handed me over? What were her thoughts like that moment when she turned and walked out of the room, knowing she would never see me again? Some of these things that lie so heavily on my mind I may never have an answer to. I can only pray that God blessed her with a peace of mind that day, and every day of her life after that.

Having three children of my own makes me realize even more how precious the gift of life is that she gave to me. The gift of life, the gift of unselfishness, and the gift of her love has surpassed any other thing she could have ever given me. I can only pray that on this Mothers' Day that our Heavenly Father will pour out His blessings upon her, and that she will be filled with more peace and hope than what she ever imagined to be possible. I can only hope that the prayers of the daughter whom she has never known will reach to the Heavenly skies, and that God will hear each and every prayer that was lifted up on her behalf.

Someone that I became very close to in my life at one time went through this same exact situation. She, too, knew the child she was carrying would have a better life with someone else. I wanted so much to take away her pain, but all I could do was ask God to give me the words that would reassure her that her decision to put her baby up for adoption was the right one. As I was writing this poem, my heart grew heavier and heavier. It was the first time in my life that I could even begin to experience what my biological mother was feeling nearly fifty years ago.

Dear God, Please Bless My Mommy

Please bless my mommy with joy and love
And put peace within her heart,
I know it wasn't easy for her
To decide that we should part.

I know how much she loves me
Because she gave life to me,
She could have chosen another path
And not even considered me.

I am so glad that You were there
To help her to decide,
And to reassure her lovingly
That You would be her guide.

For I was born a child of Yours
Blessed and created from above,
I know that You sent me to this earth
To share Your joy and love.

And though she could not raise me
She prayed that You would find,
Special parents to take care of me
Who were gentle, loving and kind.

So please, Dear God, here I am
With a big favor to ask of You,
Can You please give my mommy strength
When she is sad and blue?

Can You whisper to her everyday
That I will be alright,
Because You'll send Your angels
To watch over me day and night.

Please wipe her tears if they start to fall
And send her all Your peace and love,
Please bless her each and everyday
And watch over her from above.

And each year on my birthday
When she quietly thinks of me,
Please place a smile upon her face
And let her heart feel calm and free.

And someday, if You should decide
To bring our hearts together,
Please fill our hearts with so much love
That nothing else will matter.

Thank You, God!

My heart cried a lot of tears while I was writing that poem. Tears for my friend who I knew had a heart that was just weeping inside, and also tears for my biological mother because I knew this is how I have felt during my life towards her. I saw both sides and I knew that God gave me these words as comfort to my friend and myself. I can only pray that throughout my friend's life she will read these words, and know that there is a child out there praying for her.

God blessed me with my adoptive mother, named Virginia. Her name means "pure one." "Blessed are the pure in heart: for they shall see God," Matthew 5:8. God called my mother home nearly ten years ago, and I know that she sees God each and every day. She was the pure one; an angel of God sent here to become my mother and my best friend. I have heard before that a parent cannot be a child's best friend, but I have to disagree with that. She was everything to me, and more. I sometimes wonder how I could have ever deserved to have someone so special be my mother.

I look back now and realize even more today how special she really was. Mom was always there for Steve and me. I never saw her drink because she never did. I never heard her say an unkind word about anyone, and I never heard her swear or see her ever lose her temper. I sometimes wonder how anyone could have been that composed all those years, but I feel in my heart that God really did take those five months to find me the perfect parents. My mother was definitely the perfect mother.

The older I get, I realize that my mother probably cried more tears for me than what I will ever know. I know now, that everytime your child cries, your heart cries too. Everytime they face a difficulty in their life, you face it too. My mom always stood behind me no matter what. I know I made some wrong decisions in my life, but I don't remember her ever criticizing me. Instead she tried to help me learn from them. She supported me when I became fearful, she encouraged me when I felt I was falling apart, and she always reminded me that there was a reason why everything happens. I know now that she was right.

She was a convert to the Catholic faith when she and my dad were married. I think that it was her faith in God, and the faith that she shared so openly with my father, that made her such a remarkable woman. Maybe that is the reason why I have always needed God so much in my life because I knew that's how Mom got through her rough times. Her love for my father was so obvious. She was a devoted and loving wife and a devoted and loving mother also. The thing that I remember most of my mother was her sitting at the sewing machine for hours sewing clothes for me to wear to school. I always felt so special because she spent so much time doing things for me that maybe not all other Mothers would do. She also cooked and cleaned and kept our house so tidy and neat.

My mother always told me not to criticize anyone unless I had walked a mile in their shoes. Maybe that's the reason I have always played the part of the defender, because that is how she taught me. Her love for neighbor and friend was faithful and honest. She was truly a remarkable woman of God.

I learned to depend on her for everything. Now I sometimes think that I depended on her for too much. I rarely ever remember going to bed at night without calling her to say goodnight and to tell her I loved her. That was even after I was grown with a family of my own. Then in October of 1990, everything changed. She had a stroke, and then a month later another followed, and then finally in February of 1991, she had the one that would put her into the nursing home. Life was never the same after that. My father never missed a day of going to see her unless he was really sick himself, and I never did either.

God called her home on November 8, 1993. It was my daughter Christie's 19th birthday. When I called her at college that evening to wish her a happy birthday, the first thing she asked was how Grandma Ginny was. I told her that Grandma had given her a beautiful gift for her birthday, because the angels came to take her to Heaven, and that her suffering was now over. We cried together over the phone as if we could feel each other's hugs. The boys were doing homework at the table when I told them, and Marjoe ran upstairs and slammed the bathroom door shut as hard as he could and Ian just sat at the table and cried. My heart was filled with as much sadness for my children as it was for me.

I started writing a letter to my mom as her final days on earth were getting closer. Here is the letter I wrote and ended up reading at her funeral. It was my last way of thanking her for all that she had done for me.

November 7, 1993

Dear Mom,

As I sit here in the nursing home watching you sleep, I wonder how much longer you can keep fighting. It's been nearly three years since a stroke took away your quality of life. I never thought I'd ask you to quit fighting, but now I've told you that you can. You have fought so hard, you have pulled through times that not even the doctors thought you would, and all because of us. Now I realize it is time for you to rest.

As I watch you, I look back on my life and wonder how I could have been so fortunate to have you for a mother. The birth of a child is a miracle in itself. The birth of a child who is going to be given up for adoption, and who is going to have parents chosen by God, is an even greater miracle. I can't imagine how Steve and I deserved to be so blessed that God would give you to us as our mother.

I could write a book on what it was like to have a perfect Mother, but the book would never end.

When we were little you were always there to read us stories out of a children's nursery rhyme book. Then as we grew and the cuts and scrapes began, you were there with the band-aids. But more important, with a kiss and hug which of course you made us actually believe made the ouchy go away.

The teenage years brought us all the support that we needed. You and dad never missed a ballgame or a dance recital. You were always there for everything. All the children that ran in and out of our home started claiming you as their mom too. You always had a hug for all of them and you always made them feel at home. I remember so many of my friends couldn't believe how close we were and how well we got along. I remember telling you some of my secrets that even some of my best friends didn't know about. Some of the things that Steve and I used to tell you would just shock our friends. "I can't believe you told your mom that" they would say.

We'd answer with, "We tell her everything, she's cool!"

If I live forever, in my mind I'll still have the picture of you at the sewing machine. I could step off the school bus on Wednesday and tell you I needed a new outfit for Friday night, and by Thursday you would have one ready for me to try on. My drillteam (marching unit in high school) will probably never forget all the outfits you made that one year. Voluntarily I might add. Your crocheting for many years made many beautiful afghans for people to enjoy.

You had so much love and patience with us. I don't ever remember if you ever lost your temper, except one time on Steve's birthday when dad and he decided to play catch with a basketball in the house. When it accidentally ended up in the middle of the cake, I do recall you being a little upset.

Besides being a perfect Mother, you proved to be a perfect grandma also. Going to Grandma Ginny's house seemed to be the grandchildren's favorite place to be. You always had Little Debbies and their favorite juices ready for them when they came. They felt so important when they'd sit in your chair with you and you would read to them. Of course, if they'd stay all night, you'd rub their backs until they'd fall asleep.

You were always so proud of each of them. The front of your refrigerator was always full of the newspaper clippings that you would cut out when one of them would be in it. The love and support you so easily gave to Steve and me, you also gave to your grandchildren. You would go to all of their games, plays, and recitals. You spoiled them rotten and they loved every minute of it! You gave them more love than any amount of money could ever buy. They will never forget their loving Grandma Ginny. You brought so much sunshine into their lives that their hearts will be warmed forever.

When the time comes that I have to say goodbye, I know it's going to be the hardest thing I have ever done in my entire life. You have been my mother, my teacher, my very best friend, and my supporter for forty-years. You have given me love every day of my life, you have been there every time I have needed you, and have encouraged and inspired me with your unending faith in me. You have made me believe in myself, and you have helped deepen my faith. How can I ever thank you enough for everything you have done for me?

Taking me to church as a child and teaching me to believe that God helps us to get through anything is the greatest gift that you and dad have ever given me.

November 10, 1993

It has been three days since I wrote that part of your tribute. I know that you are in Heaven because I was there when the angels came to take you. It was Christie's 19th birthday. The sun had shone bright that day and it had set to allow the stars to shine bright in the darkened sky. I said the "Our Father" as your soul started to leave and you took your last breath on the "Amen." It was the most peaceful and comforting moment that I have ever been able to share with you. In my heart it was a prayer answered. You were there with me every minute of my entire life and I had asked God to let me be with you at that miraculous moment. The presence of the angels coming was something that I can't explain, I could only feel it.

The need to call you and chat, to hug you and give you a kiss will never end. But I know that you are in Heaven, and God is holding you in the palm of His hand. The rainbows have no end, the stars forever twinkle, and the sun will shine forever in your new home.

You have been the perfect wife, mother and grandmother and now God has blessed you. Your love will always be in our hearts for all eternity. I know that you have not died; you have only traveled to the ultimate blue Heavens and have become an angel of God. Now I have my very own guardian angel, who protected me as a mother here, and who will continue to protect me as an angel from above.

We love you and we will never quit missing you, but we will feel your presence everyday of our remaining lives.

Your voice will whisper to us in the wind, your love will warm us through the sun, and the moon will forever shine bright.

Goodbye Mom, at least for now. Keep watching for me because someday my hand will be reaching for yours, and I know that will be waiting for me.

I'll love you forever.

That first year after mom's death seemed to be the worst year I had ever experienced in my life. I tried so hard to stay strong for my father, who was lost without her. He was seventy-eight at the time, and had been with my mother for the last forty four years of his life. I tried so hard to stay strong for my children, who I knew had breaking hearts also. Victor (who was my fiancé at the time) and I started fighting all the time. He could not understand my pain, and I was bitter because he couldn't. I lost track of me, and became consumed with the grief. I remember going to the cemetary and kneeling in snow and crying until the tears were frozen to my face. I convinced myself that if I knelt there long enough, she would appear for one last hug. I felt like no one in the world could possibly feel the pain that had overtaken me. When my mother was here, she would always assure me that things would work out. Now she was no longer here, and I too, was lost. I felt like my heart would never get over the pain of losing her. I cried more tears then I thought were possible. It took a long time before I could hear the word "mother" without falling apart, but God is true to His word. He helped my sorrowful heart to heal, and He filled me with compassion for anyone who has lost a mother.

Now for Mother's Day, all I can do is remember the times we spent together and thank God that I was able to share the first forty years of my life with someone so special. I ran across a poem that I wrote her one year for Mother's Day, but yet there was no date on it. I suppose when I wrote it, time didn't matter because these feelings had lived inside of my being the whole time I was growing up.

Mothers' Day

You've given me everything I needed
Since the day you took me home,
And you've always been at my side
Never leaving me alone.

You taught me how to cry and laugh
And how to love and care,
And most important you taught me how
To give my love to others to share.

You've been at my side through happy and sad
And left your arms always open for me,
And because of all the love you gave
You made my world a beautiful place to be.

So what more can I say today
Then Happy Mothers' Day with love,
And may God bless you everyday
With His graces from above.

Today, as I read that poem on this Mothers' Day, I realize that my life has never been the same since she left her earthly home, but the memories that we shared will live forever in my heart. God truly blessed me when He picked her out to be my mother. I know that I now have my very own guardian angel who watches over me from Heaven's gate, and I know she is smiling as I write this book. She knew years before I did, that this was the job that God wanted me to do. Happy Mothers' Day, Mom, I love you!

ISAIAH 66:13

"AS A MOTHER COMFORTS HER SON SO WILL I COMFORT YOU."

REFLECTION:

It takes someone very special to be a mother. Who in your life can you thank God for, who has been a loving mother, or like a mother to you?

Dear Heavenly Father

You gave to me two mothers. You sent me a mother who would carry me and give birth to me, and then one who would raise me as her very own. Thank You for blessing me so much in my life. Please help all those right now who are carrying the gift of life inside of them, and who are frightened of what the future holds for them. Guide them on the path to make the right decision about that life, and then send them a peace in their heart so they will never question their decision. In the most precious name of Your Son, Jesus Christ. Amen.

My Father's Love

As the sun shines brilliantly in the sky today, I will ask our Heavenly Father to bless all the fathers out there on this Fathers' Day. Today is a very special day for me to give thanks to my Heavenly Father above. He chose a very unique and loving man to be my father. I have been so blessed in my life because of my father's love, and I wish that I was able to share that love with so many children out there who have not been as blessed as I have been.

Long before my conception, God already knew who He would choose to become my father, and to raise me as his very own daughter. I don't know if my biological father knew of my mother's pregnancy with me or not, and chances are I may never know. I do know that God had His hand in it, and that I came to be a very important person in my father's life. Dad always tells everyone that they should all have a "Mary," but my response is that everyone should have a dad like mine. His name is Cletus, but everyone calls him "Hinie." I can't even remember the story of how that name came about, but that's how everyone knows him.

Growing up on the farm came to be a very special time for me when I bonded very closely with my dad. I seemed to enjoy being out in the barn, and out in the fields instead of in the house doing "girl stuff." I can remember so clearly riding the tractor in the fields with dad, and helping him farm. I remember a mile or so down the road from where we lived, he owned a lot of farmland. We would work the field until we would have to take a break, and then we would sit under the old walnut tree that would provide relief from the hot sun, and we would drink our cool water from the thermos we had taken along. Tractors back then had no coverings on them, let alone air conditiong in the cab, so farming was a very hot job in the summer. I can remember riding in the wagon on the way to town to take the grain in, and how exciting it was to know that all that grain had come from a hard day's work with my dad. There was a little old grocery store right across from the mill, and if my brother and I had been really good that day, dad would take us in the store to get us a treat. We would usually get a bottle of cream soda too. The store had a wooden floor in it, and it would always squeak when we would walk in. Those are the happy times I remember sharing with my dad, as a child.

Dad was the type of man who always made time for his family. As I grew up, and became involved in a lot of activities, I remember that dad somehow always found the time to go to something that was important to me. I took tap dance for nearly ten years. Once a year we would have a dance recital. It seemed as though dad was always busy in the fields with the crops or in the barn taking care of the animals, yet he always found the time to go see me. I can even remember running out to the field on a Saturday afternoon to tell dad it was time for me to leave for the parade because my drillteam was marching. He would always tell me that he would see me there. I know now since I've gotten older, exactly how much the farmers depend on good weather to get their farming done by their deadline. I wonder sometimes if dad ever got behind in those days because he gave up all of a Saturday to go watch me march in a parade. If he did, he never told me.

Dad was always there to tell Steve and me what a good job we were doing, and to encourage us if we felt unworthy of his praises. I don't remember him ever critizing us in anything we did. I'm sure that growing up through the teen years, there were times that he thought about shaking me silly once in a while, but he never did. Dad raised us to believe that if we got in trouble in school we would get in trouble when we got home. In third grade, I got a spanking from one of the "Sisters" at my St. Mary's School for crawling under the bathroom door instead of walking through it. I don't even know why I did it. When I got home, I told mom I had gotten into trouble, and she told me she would have to tell dad when he got home. I remember being really scared because of the promise dad had always made. I lay awake that night waiting on him to get home from second shift. When mom told him what had happened, I can still remember him laughing, as he said, "That sounds like our Mary." I knew I could easily fall asleep now, as the news had already been broken, and I knew I wasn't going to get into trouble. The next morning, I remember him calling me down to the kitchen and saying, "I heard you got into a little trouble at school". In the back of my mind, I recalled his laughter the night before when mom told him, but I couldn't let on that I knew, so I went along with him. Needless to say, I did not get a spanking at home.

My dad was a perfect role model as far as a husband and father. I never heard him and mom fight, and I often wondered if they ever did, but somehow, I really don't think so. Dad was always there for us, and he raised us in a loving, God-filled home, which made me understand what a family was all about.

I know that he did not approve of my first marriage, and I'm sure that he knew back then that it would not work, but he never told me what to do. He let me make my own decisions, and then he was there to pick me up when I fell flat on my face. That loving father image that he portrayed helped me to sense God as my loving Father also. It was easy for me to be able to understand God's love for me, and for all of His children. Knowing that my dad was always there for me no matter what, led me to believe that God would also be there for me under any circumstance. My dad never stayed mad about anything, I don't even remember him getting upset. So I could always picture my Heavenly Father being the same way. I could never imagine God getting mad at me, or ever reminding me that I had done wrong. I only pictured Him being there when I made a mistake, and He would pick me up and carry me as I cried through my heartache. It was so easy for me to relate to my father's love, and therefore, I grew up knowing God's unconditional love for me was as easy to receive as was my own father's. My life has been so blessed because of my father's love, and also because of my Heavenly Father's love.

As long as I live, I will always remember the most important lesson in life that my father ever taught me. It is the same lesson that his father taught him while growing up. My dad always says, "Honey, my dad always said to me, don't ever give up the faith, son, don't ever give up the faith." I truly believe that my grandpa instilled that in my dad's heart at a very young age, and I was fortunate enough to have my dad pass that advice on to me as I was growing up. I have heard him say it so often, and I have also seen him live it. He has never given up in life, and I know he has endured his share of struggles and pain, but he never gave up. His faith in God has been strong, and he has walked the walk and talked the talk.

I wrote a poem for church years ago about a father. While I wrote it, I reflected on my own father and how fortunate I was that my dad was all these things to me.

A Father Is....

A father is a loving man
Who loves his children the best he can,
He teaches them love instead of hate
He teaches them patience and how to wait.

He helps them to learn right from wrong
He offers them his hand which is oh, so strong,
He gives them encouragement along the way
He instills in them the faith to face each day.

He sets an example of what honesty means
He helps them to reach into a future of dreams,
He stands behind them straight and tall
He helps them back up if they start to fall.

He praises them daily with confidence and pride
He teaches them security never leaving their side,
He teaches them of God from the very start
He loves them with all the depth of his heart.

Sometimes I wish I could run out into the world, and give to every child out there, a true father in their life. I was so blessed, and I know that often all children are not as fortunate as I was. I do know for certain that every child in this entire world was placed here for a very specific reason, and that they do have a true and loving Father up above who will watch over them each day of their life. God is there to take their hand and guide their way through their life. He is there to carry them through the storms of life when the wind is blowing so hard they can no longer walk on their own. He is there to fill their heart with peace and to put laughter into their soul. Every child in this world deserves a loving and faithful father. All children in this world have God, who is waiting very patiently for them to call upon Him, and tell Him that He is needed in their lives. He wants to be our Father, our guide, our supporter and our strength.

I was blessed on this earth with three fathers, my Heavenly Father up above, my biological father who gave me life, and my father who raised me as his very own daughter. He is the one who taught me of God's love and faithfulness, and he taught me to never give up in life. He gave me the same unselfish love that God gives to each one of us. He gave me his time, his friendship, and the most important gift of all, his gift of faith. The love of my dad is as close to my Heavenly Father's love as what I could ever imagine. God is our Father, and He has so many gifts that He wants to give us, all we have to do is ask for them. If we open our hearts to Him, we will have the gift of His love, and we will need nothing else in our lives. A father's love is a precious gift.

<u>JOHN 5:19</u>

"JESUS ANSWERED AND SAID TO THEM, "AMEN, AMEN, I SAY TO YOU, A SON CANNOT DO ANYTHING ON HIS OWN, BUT ONLY WHAT HE SEES HIS FATHER DOING, FOR WHAT HE DOES, HIS SON WILL DO ALSO."

<u>REFLECTION:</u>

A father's love is essential in the growth of mind and soul. Can you thank someone today for his father like love, and for sharing with you the love of your Heavenly Father above?

Dear Heavenly Father

I was blessed with a father who raised me in Your love and guidance. It has been so easy for me to grasp the concept of a Heavenly Father's care because of my dad. Thank You for the father You chose for me. May You bless all those children who weren't as fortunate. Please let them feel Your love as their Father, and remind them that You will always be there to love them as a father should. You will never leave a child of Yours fatherless. In the most precious name of Your Son, Jesus Christ. Amen.

The Family That Prays Together

Do you remember the old saying, "The family that prays together stays together?" While I was growing up, it seems as though I heard that saying all the time. Now that I am older it has taken on a real meaning in my life.

My family did pray a lot. We went to church together; we prayed at home, and we prayed in the car. I remember my mother praying when it would storm out, asking God for protection for our family. She was always so scared of storms. I grew up relying on prayer for a lot of my needs, but never did I fully realize how very true that statement was until I grew older.

I was married at the age of 20 to a guy I had a crush on throughout part of my high school years. His name was Robin. I continued to go to church after I was married, but our beliefs were so much different when it came to the subject of faith. He too, had been raised Catholic, but quit going to church when he got in high school. Here I was remembering back to my childhood and just assumed that all families went to church together. I found out very quickly that it doesn't always happen that way.

Throughout ten years of marriage, and the birth of our three children, I can't remember his ever going to church with me. We had all the children baptized when they were infants, which he did attend those ceremonies. We used to argue all the time about why I went to church and why he didn't. He used to ask me how I knew for sure that there was a God up there. I used to ask him how he knew for sure that there wasn't. This brought about in me a very defensive nature. One night after we had argued over this very issue, I again wrote my thoughts out on paper. Here were the words that night that seemed to be the answer to his question.

If God Really Isn't Up There

If God really isn't up there
Watching over us day by day,
Then who do you think is guiding us
And showing us the right way?

Do you really think that the sun above
With all of its glorious shine,
Just happened to fall in place one day
Whenever it felt it was time?

I look up and see the radiant full moon
And I shiver from head to toe,
Can you really say that one of us
Made that beautiful moon with its glow?

We walk through nature everyday
Shuffling through leaves and breathing fresh air,
And you're honestly trying to tell me
there's no one up there who really cares?

Well, you believe what you want to
And I'll believe in God's love,
And I'll keep praying everyday
That soon, you'll turn to Him above.

I wanted so much for him to share that same faith with me, to go to church and sit with us as a family, but that day never came. After ten years of marriage our relationship ended, and we divorced. I felt as though I had failed in some way. I even started doubting myself and what I really believed in. Some nights I would go out into my backyard and just stare at that full moon, and I would say, "God, where are you, can you hear me crying for you?"

I knew that prayer had been a part of my life since my beginning, and now all of a sudden I wondered if God had heard me pleading for my marriage to work. I wondered where God was when I would go to bed at night not knowing where my husband was or even if he was alright. I wondered where God was when I prayed for my husband to quit partying year after year, and yet my love and prayers didn't seem to be enough to make a difference. I knew in my heart that God was still there for me, I just didn't understand why He was so silent. Why hadn't my prayers been heard and answered? Why couldn't He see my pain, and take away the things that were causing it? I just could not understand any of it.

"In God's time" we always hear, and we have to be patient until that time is right. Little did I know then, that today I would be remarried to a wonderful man who chose to go to church with me on our first date, instead of waiting to pick me up when I got home. God knew when I was sitting out in my backyard crying that He would send me someone to share my faith with someday.

They say that "God works in mysterious ways," and I know for sure that is true. Victor, my husband now, was an assistant at the factory where I started working even before my divorce. He and I never got along too well back then. It seemed as though he thought I talked too much, and I was always getting in trouble by him. I felt like he enjoyed showing his authority and he thought I enjoyed doing things to make him mad.

One time when he told me he didn't want to see me talking the rest of the day, I put a big piece of masking tape on my mouth, drew a red smiley face on it, and continued to walk around glaring at him everytime he looked at me. My lead lady Paula eventually told me I'd better take it off, or I would be in the office. Victor and I had several confrontations that were similar.

During this time in my life is when I went through my divorce. After my divorce from Robin, I only dated one guy and his name was Ralph. Our communication was wonderful. I did not know until Ralph came along, that two people could actually carry on a conversation for hours. It felt so good to be able to share my pain and my laughter with someone who really cared about me. Fighting every feeling I could, I finally gave in and fell in love. Two years later, he would develop a brain tumor and a year after that, Jesus took him home.

I was devastated. I had finally taken a chance on love again, and then I lost him. I remember sitting on his car only minutes after I had held his hand as he died. I looked up at the sky sobbing, and asked God why He had to take him. I was so mad at God; I didn't know what to do. I felt like He had ignored my pleas once again. I had prayed earnestly for a full recovery of Ralph's cancer, and my prayers were not heard. Why was this happening? Why did He allow someone I loved to be ripped out of my hands?

I was lost, heartbroken, and ready to give up on everything. I cried myself to sleep every night. I went to work in a daze. I was raising three children on my own and was barely able to keep my own spirits up, let alone theirs. Every weekend I would buy a six pack of beer, and drink three beers on Friday night after the children went to bed, and the other three on Saturday night. For me that was a lot of beer, because I had never been much of a drinker. My mother became worried about me. I knew I was slipping deeper and deeper into a state of sadness, which I had no control over. I knew my mother was praying for me to find some peace, somewhere.

That's when Victor came along. The person whom I never dreamed would ever have a place in my life, and there we were dating. He had two daughters, so together we had five children. Our children got along very well, and things were wonderful. The thought of ever marrying again absolutely terrified me though. It would be six years before we would walk down the aisle as husband and wife.

I still think the one thing that attracted him to me was his response when he asked me out for the first time. I told him that my children and I went to church every Saturday night, and that I would not miss. I told him he could either pick me up before church and go with us, or wait till after I got home. He said he'd pick us up before. For the first time in my life I had a man beside of me in church, and I admired him for that. That prayer of many years ago had finally been answered. It was worth the wait! Victor not only went to church with me, but ended up being a singer for church also. He attended other church activities, and was very open to anything that my faith had to offer him. I knew that this marriage would work without a doubt, because God was a part of it. That is all that a marriage needs, God and two people who are willing to listen to what He tells them. He will only continue to bring them closer and closer as time goes on.

"The family that prays together stays together." My parents were right when they said that. I look at the people in my church now, and most of them I know a lot that has happened in their lives, just as the Dietsches. I know that a lot of them have had their share of sorrow and grief, whether it was a death in the family, financial stress, children straying, loss of jobs, fires, and many other tragic happenings that people go through. But one thing that stands true is they were able to get through the tough times, and still stand tall together. Knowing that God is working in a marriage makes it easier to believe that a family can get through anything.

As our children grew, there became many obstacles in our own marriage. Whenever there is a mixed family, there is bound to be some resistance somewhere. Victor and I had our shares of ups and downs. There were many times when the road was rough, and it would have been so easy to give up. Sometimes the resistance seemed more than we could handle. We have shared as many tears as we have laughter, during the dating years and along with the married years. We buried our mothers on the same day one year apart. We have dealt with children going down the wrong path and making bad choices. We have gone through teenage pregnancies, financial problems, sickness, and loss of jobs; but one thing that has helped us through it all is the fact that every week we sat together in God's home asking Him for help through the storms of life, and thanking Him for always being there no matter what. Victor even ended up accepting the position of "Spiritual Director" for the men's Christ Renews His Parish team. That year his faith grew even stronger, and our marriage became closer to God also.

I learned a lot when I grew up in my church community. Over the years I watched the trials that families were going through, but yet I watched them grow stronger through it all.

I knew of two people who had gone through some tough times going through their divorces, and then God brought them together to share their lives as one. They asked me to write a poem for them and read it at their wedding. Again, I asked God to help me write something that would be His message to them. These are the words that He gave to me. This was for my dear friends, Laurie and Nick.

God's Union Of Two

A marriage made in heaven
Is created by God above,
He searches and finds two hearts and souls
And unites them both in love.

He promises to be with them
As He guides them along their way,
He sends joy and peace to fill their hearts
And laughter with each day.

He gives them strength in times of need
And never lets them down,
He sends them daily little signs
To remind them He's always around.

If they put their faith in Him
And trust Him with each new day,
Their lives will forever be as one
And be blessed in every way.

For God has promised to all of us
Who make Him the head of our home,
Our journey on this path of life
Will never be spent alone.

For He will give us sunshine
To warm our hearts with love,
And rainbows as a promise
To watch over us from above.

On this your special wedding day
As your marriage has just begun,
Thank God for the blessings He's given
As He unites you both as one.

Each morning as the sun comes up
Thank Him for being together,
Say a prayer as you go to sleep
And He'll bless your marriage forever.

I felt when I was writing that poem that God was trying to remind me that sometimes we try and pick our own partners for life, but it doesn't always work. If we let God do the choosing of finding two hearts and souls, chances are we will stay together. We will walk through the storms of life together, and through the sunny days together, but we will always walk hand in hand, and God will be our guide leading us on our journey of love.

"THE LORD GOD SAID: IT IS NOT GOOD FOR THE MAN TO BE ALONE. I WILL MAKE A SUITABLE PARTNER FOR HIM."

REFLECTION:

Witnessing what God can do in a relationship can be powerful. Who can you look at and know that God is truly in their lives, and has been the glue that kept their marriage together?

Dear Heavenly Father

I have been so blessed with being raised in a family that prayed together through every generation. Thank You for being there as I raised my own children, and taught them to pray. I know that as long as You are the head of a family, and they walk their journey of faith with You guiding them, they will stay united. Please touch the hearts of those families who don't know You, and bring them close to You. In the most precious name of Your Son, Jesus Christ. Amen.

Lord, Bless My Child

Anyone who is a parent knows the joy and laughter, pain and trials that go into being a parent. I always dreamed when I was young, of falling in love, getting married, and then making the decision with my husband to start a family. I could picture the two of us sitting side by side, gazing into each other's eyes, telling one another that it was time to have a baby. That dream never happened. Sex before marriage can take away a lot of dreams that will never take place. I became a parent alright, but it wasn't the fairytale surrounding that I had dreamed of while growing up. I, along with many other young adults, never thought that I would be the one who would get caught. I was twenty years old at the time, and Robin and I had been seeing each other off and on for the past six years. It all started with that junior high crush on each other. I had been taught while growing up in my Catholic faith that sex should be saved until marriage. I honored that throughout all of my high school years, but then after I graduated, Robin and I were together one evening the next spring, and it happened. I can't remember ever feeling so guilty about anything in my entire life. That night would be the night that would change the fate of my entire life. I wish there was some way now that I could make young adults see how this decision can affect their lives. I knew that I had let myself down, and I knew that if my parents ever found out, they would be heart broken. I could barely stand the thought that God knew also, that a very important part of me had just been shared with someone else.

A year later, I found out that I was pregnant. I was still with Robin, and I truly loved him, but it was not the romantic relationship that I wanted. He was upset when I told him of my pregnancy. I was upset with myself for not being more careful. Our parents started fighting, and it seemed as though nothing would ever work out right. We were married three months later, and within six months our daughter Christie was born.

My mother had always told me that my dad was a very attentive and loving father as Steve and I were growing up. I expected Robin to be the same way. I was very disappointed when it didn't happen that way. I had received a lot from my father, and I expected a lot from Robin. I started wondering if I was actually expecting too much.

Between 1974 and 1981, we had our three children. Christie was born in 1974, Marjoe in 1979, and Ian in 1981. Being twenty-eight years old and being a mother to three children seemed to take a lot of patience and love. When Robin and I weren't getting along, which was most of the time, I would sit and hang on to my children as if to never let go. My love for them grew stronger every day. I felt the guilt of not giving to them the kind of father that I had, and I did everything I could to make it up to them. I became their mother, father, and their friend. My daughter and I developed a very close relationship from the very beginning. She and I were always spending time together, as the boys were only two years apart, and they would play and sometimes fight for hours on end.

When their father and I divorced after ten years of marriage, Christie had just turned ten a few weeks before the divorce was final. Marjoe was five, and Ian was three. I knew that life was not going to be easy, but I also knew that God would be there to help me through it. I look back now, and if I had not had my parents, along with God to depend on, I don't know if I would have survived. Working full time to support them and having enough energy to go to the games and school functions seemed to take a lot of stamina. Whenever I needed any pep talks, my mom was there to give them to me.

I became so very much in love with all my children, it seemed as though they were the reason I kept going at times. I knew that they depended on me for everything, and I wanted to give them everything I possibly could. We didn't have much material wise, but we had all the love and laughter that we needed.

I would tuck them in bed every single night of their lives. We would read bedtime stories, and then we would say our prayers. Sometimes we would have to pray for so many people that the prayers would seem to never end. I always felt good after I would tuck them in. I knew that God would hear our prayers for all of our loved ones, and I knew that I was helping to teach them what my parents had taught me. God was there at all times just waiting on us to call, and we could talk to Him about anything. We would thank Him during our prayers for all of the things that He did for us, and for all that we had. We would also pour out our heartaches to Him when we were crying inside. I tried so hard to teach them of His unconditional love and His never ending faithfulness. I never had a thought that someday they may question His presence in their lives. But unfortunately, that someday did come.

Taking three children to church every week by myself seemed to be a real struggle at times. There were times when I would leave after Mass and wonder what the sermon had been about. Sometimes I even wondered if my being there had actually counted. Other people would reassure me that God was happy with me for "trying" so hard to raise them in the faith. Maybe that's the reason why I tell mothers with children now, that it's good to see them in church. I know sometimes a mother will be upset over the way their child is acting, and I will reassure them that God is happy they are there.

Throughout the years of raising them, there were not too many times that we did not make it to church. I wanted my children to have that security that I had been raised with. I did not get too much resistance from them until after my mother died. My daughter had just started college a few months earlier, and continued to go to church when it fit into her schedule, which sometimes was not too often. But my boys on the other hand, were really starting to rebel at any thought of the 'religious' theme. They were twelve and fourteen at the time, and we had prayed for grandma's healing every night for nearly three years after her stroke. After her death I realized that we had finally had our prayers answered, because I knew that there is no greater healing then to be taken home to live with our Heavenly Father. But to three grandchildren who absolutely adored their precious grandma, it seemed to be something that a loving God would not let happen. Christie was at college to grieve by herself, and to bury herself in her studies and her job. The boys though decided to take different paths to deal with their grief. Somehow, they got off on the wrong road, and I learned to depend on God more than I ever had in my entire life. Victor and I were fighting all the time because of it. Since he had never had any boys of his own, He didn't know how to handle mine either. The relationship they had when the boys were young was no longer there. I was in a battle I couldn't win, and I felt like I was all by myself.

The more my boys turned away, and the more fights Victor and I had, the more time I spent going into the silence of God's home to cry my heart out. I was losing them all, and I had no idea how to stop it from happening. Marjoe, the oldest son, completely changed his friends and the music he listened to. It seemed as though everything that I raised him with, he started to rebel against. The morning after his fifteenth birthday, at 2:35 a.m., I was sitting at my kitchen table wondering if he was alright, where he was, and if he would make it home. My mind wandered back to the times when he was little, and I wrote the following thoughts as I waited into the depth of the morning.

Where Is My Son

He was once a little boy, mommy's little boy,
with blond hair, and sparkling blue eyes,
and a halo around his head.
I'd hold him so close, rocking him in the rocking chair,
and stare deeply into his innocent eyes,
wondering what he was thinking.
I'd sing to him, my made up song just for him,
"Don't you cry my little man, my little man, my little man,
don't you cry my little man, we all love you.
guess I'll have to keep singing all night,
singing all night, singing all night,

guess I'll have to keep singing all night,
so you will not cry."
And slowly, his eyelids would close,
till he was sound asleep.
But that was long ago.......
He was once a little boy, who would sit for hours,
playing with matchbox cars, and zooming them up and down
over his make believe hills.
He'd run up to me, with his favorite storybook,
and say, "mommy, will you read this book to me?"
And we'd go sit down, and read the same book,
over and over again.
But that was long ago.........
He was once a little boy, who would hold on tight to my hand,
wherever we would go, as to not ever wanting to be separated.
And if he fell, and got a cut or scrape, he'd run to me
with tears in his eyes saying, "Mommy, make my ouchy go away."
And with a simple magical kiss, somehow, he honestly thought
it disappeared, and he in return, would give me a big hug and kiss,
saying, "I love you this much," with arms spread apart
as far as he could reach them, and then off he would run.
But that was long ago........
He was once a little boy, who would come from school,
and tell me everything that happened the whole entire day.
He'd have friends over to play, and we'd all go outside,
and play ball in the yard on a bright and sunny day,
He'd smile and be so happy, without a care in the world.
But that was long ago.....
He was once a little boy, who would go to church with me,
every Saturday night,
And take with him his storybooks about God, and "Prayers for Children",
and he'd sit on my lap in church saying, with a question in his eyes,
"Where is Jesus?", and I would try to explain to him,
but yet his eyes would tell me that he did not fully understand.
Sometimes he would fall asleep in my arms, for the whole Mass,
and I'd wake him up when it was time to go.

Then later on in the evening, I would tuck him in bed,
and he would say to me, "Don't forget my nighty night prayers".
We would pray for all our friends and family,
and then I'd pull up his blankets, give him a big hug and kiss, and say,
"Good night mommy loves you, God bless you, see you tomorrow."
But that was long ago......
What happened to mommy's little boy? Where did he go?
Oh, how I miss him so much!
He's a teenager now, rebellious and resentful,
he no longer needs me for anything.
I cannot hold his hand anymore, nor read him books to make him smile.
He will no longer go to church, nor talk to me about anything.
He no longer has anyone spend the night, instead he runs with friends
whom I do not even know.
He no longer thinks I'm the smartest person in the world, he thinks he is.
Nor does he think I could ever make the pain go away.
His eyes are no longer innocent; there is no halo around his head,
and his heart and spirit no longer live here.
He doesn't talk to me like he used too.
He doesn't so easily say, "I love you."
And there are no more bear hugs making me feel like I am the most
important person in his world.
Where is my little boy?
I'm not really sure.
I can only pray that someday, he will be here again.
But until then, I can only pray.
I can only pray, that the morals and values that I taught him
when he was so young, will someday again surface.
I can only pray, that the unselfish love that I gave to him,
will someday reassure him, just how important he is in my life.
I can only pray, that during this rebellious stage,
he will never forget that God and I are here for him,
just as we always were when he was growing up.
I can only pray, that he finds himself going down the right path in life,
remembering right from wrong, with the right friends at his side,
so his life will be full of sunshine and rainbows,

instead of cloudy and rainy days.
I can only pray, that my little boy will come back to me,
someday, as a loving and caring young man,
and our love and closeness will again be,
as it was so long ago,
when he was "mommy's little boy."

I did not know when I wrote that, I would be giving a copy of it to my other son a few years later. I felt them slipping right out of my hands, and no matter how hard I tried to change things, nothing seemed to work. It was through those trials and tears that I would learn so much compassion for other parents who were struggling with their teens, also.

It was through those times of frustration and questioning, that I learned to depend on God even more than I had before. It was through those sleepless nights when I learned about God's unconditional love in a way I had never known before. I had always loved my children very deeply, but sometimes it is so easy to love someone when the love is returned. I was all of a sudden faced with a situation that made me question how they could do the things they were doing, but in my heart I still loved them as much as ever, if not more, because I wanted so much to try and help them.

God loves His children no matter what we do, or how far away from Him we stray. He never quits loving us. He never gives up on us. He stays there watching us with His arms opened wide waiting for us to return. I have learned to love my children in the same way. My mother always told me there was a reason why everything happens the way it does. I know now that I will never give up on my children, just as God will never give up on me. I will continue to pray that someday, I will see each one of them come back to the faith that they were raised with. I pray that someday I will look at them, and know in my heart that they have finally found the peace that God was waiting so patiently to give them. I will pray that they will pass on that faith to their children just as my parents passed it on to me. The greatest gift a parent can give to their child is faith. Someday, I know that they will see it too.

It has been ten years since I wrote, "Where is my son?" My daughter and I are as close as we ever were, and the older she gets, she sees how important faith is to a family. She is married to her wonderful husband Eric, and they are raising my grandsons in God's love.

Ian became a father at a very young age, and has also given me two grandsons. He is a very loving and caring dad. I am so proud of him, and thankful that he knew how to be a good father.

Marjoe has grown into a responsible adult also. I am proud of all my children, and thankful the Lord watched over them as they grew. When my boys call me, and we talk for awhile, and are ready to hang up they say, "Love you." When they come to visit, I always get a bear hug, even though they are now both over six feet tall. They are still not where I pray that they will be someday, but I know that they are on their way. I believe that all of my prayers will be answered in time and God's peace will find a way into their hearts.

I know that God is true to His promises, and I know that I worked really hard in teaching them their values in life, and that the faith that I passed down to them will eventually resurface again someday. It's so easy for children to think that we, as parents, are trying to shove something down their throat when they are not ready to commit to a true relationship with our Lord. The older they get, I think they realize that it is for their own happiness and security that we want this for them. I want my children to see the sun coming up each day, with a hope that fills their heart with a peace that only God can provide. I want them to have happiness in their lives, and not have to go to every corner of the earth to find it. I will never quit praying for my children, and I will never give up on them. I'm sure God has been a little impatient with me at times, but yet He never let go of me. I will never let go of my children either.

Years ago, a close friend of mine, Nita, who lives in Texas, called and asked me to write a poem that could be used in a church cookbook that her children were putting together in school. Right away I thought of my own children. At the time she called, the teen years were getting rough. Here is the poem that I gave to her, but I think it really ended up being a prayer.

Lord, Bless My Child

Lord, bless my little baby today,
As I watch him sleep so sound,
Help him to have beautiful dreams,
Where rainbows are always found.

Lord, bless my growing toddler today.
As he learns to walk and run,
Help him to grow up in a world,
That's filled with love and fun.

Lord, bless my young child today,
As his first day of school is here,
Help him adjust and learn,
And let his heart be free of fear.

Lord, bless my curious teenager today,
As he decides what is wrong or right,
Help him to stay strong enough,
To say "No" without a fight.

Lord, bless my young man today,
As he leaves to start his new life,
Help him to choose a good partner,
Who will be a loving and Christian wife.

Lord, bless my little grandchild today...

Every generation needs prayers. God is waiting so patiently for us to pray for all of our children and their families. Someday, all of these prayers will be answered, and God's family will stretch across the oceans hand in hand, and it will be a beautiful world in which we live.

PROVERBS 22:6

"TRAIN A BOY IN THE WAY HE SHOULD GO; EVEN WHEN HE IS OLD, HE WILL NOT SWERVE FROM IT. "

REFLECTION:

We are all God's children, and He loves us equally. Have you shared His love with your own children, or with someone else's child who needs to learn about Him?

Dear Heavenly Father

It is such a huge responsibility to raise a child and be a good parent. Bless those parents who need Your love and guidance as they try so hard to guide their children on the right path. Help those children right now who are lost, and cannot seem to find their way in this world of uncertainty. Bring them close to Your heart, so that they may feel Your love deep within their being. Place Your protection around them in time of trouble. Please bless all of Your children, whether young or old, and guide them where they need to be. In the most precious name of Your Son, Jesus Christ. Amen.

A Lifetime Of Faith

I often wonder what it would be like to go back into the "olden days" and live for a short time, and then share those experiences with others who walked in those days also. I can talk to my Aunt Helen now, who was eight years old when my father was born, and somehow try to recapture what growing up in the early 1900's was like.

She was born on her parents' farm back in 1907. She is ninety five years old right now, but still remembers the innocence of our world back then. Talking to her makes it so easy to just picture the way things were back then. She says she can still remember when she was growing up, sitting down at the breakfast table every morning with her family and praying before they even took their first bite. In the evenings when it drew close to night time, she would kneel beside her bed and faithfully say her prayers each and every night.

My grandparents were Catholic, and so she was raised in a Catholic home with the old fashioned laws of fasting and abstinence before receiving Christ's Body and Blood in Communion. On Saturday nights after midnight, there was to be nothing eaten or drunk if you wanted to receive Communion the next morning at Mass. She even said that they would not even have a drop of water touch their lips during this time. To me that would be a true sacrifice. On Wednesday and Fridays of Lent they would abstain from eating meat.

They would go to church in a horse and buggy, regardless of what the weather was like. She says the neighborhood would all take turns of getting each other into town to church on Sunday mornings. In the winter, they would use one horse to pull a sleigh which would hold two people, and a bob sled would be pulled by two horses, and those would hold about six or eight people.

She even remembers her mother telling her that her great grandmother had even walked to church on Sunday to Blakeslee, which is a little town about seven miles north of where we live. What dedication to our Lord to think of someone going through that amount of work to get to a Sunday church service. I would like to believe that this generation is that dedicated also, but I'm honestly not sure. It sometimes seems that just getting up early on Sunday morning and driving to church can be an effort to some today.

My Aunt Helen was named after her grandmother Helena, and she says that people have told her what a wonderful and honest woman she was. Aunt Helen says she truly believes when her grandma died before she was born, that she became Aunt Helen's guardian angel and started to watch over her, and has continued to do so her entire life.

One time when Aunt Helen was crossing the railroad tracks in her horse and buggy, there was a train coming, but somehow she made it across the tracks just in time. She was on her way to high school that day, and has never forgotten the near-death experience in which something seemed to pull the horse and buggy ahead just in time.

Another time in her life that could have been a tragic accident seemed to have another startling end to it. She and her husband Jim were driving home from Toledo on icy roads when their car started to slide, and they ended up spinning around and ending up in the ditch. Again, she felt the presence of someone who was watching out for them and keeping them safe. Do you believe in guardian angels, because my Aunt Helen does?

Aunt Helen was baptized as an infant, and her mother received her First Communion and was confirmed on that same day. My grandma was converted to the Catholic faith when she married my grandfather, and so this was a big day in her life for her and her daughter Helen.

Going to Mass every Sunday was not a decision back then; it was just something you did. Aunt Helen says that missing Mass was not an option; it was something that you faithfully did every solid week, and you did it because you wanted to. People knew that they needed their faith strengthened, and they knew this was the way to do it. Growing into a deeper relationship with our Lord is something that people wanted to do, and they worked at it.

I love to hear her talk of riding her pony to the country school in the mornings, and opening their day at school with a prayer to God, and then singing a song to glorify His name. This was in a public school! Before the churches were built, she said that people used to gather in each other's houses and take turns holding the prayer services in their homes. I feel like people really appreciated the freedom of religion they had back then, and they were ready to thank God for it every opportunity they could find.

Neighbors were always gathering together to socialize and have fun. Aunt Helen says that they used to have a get together called a "box social" which was a gathering in which the women would decorate boxes and fill them full of meat, fresh fruit, and vegetables. They would all gather at the little school in the country and auction these boxes off to the highest bidder. The money was then used to buy things for the school that were needed. The "box social" served as two purposes. It helped raise money, and it gave people the opportunity to share joy and friendship with one another. She has also told me that when someone built a new barn, they would always hold a square dance in it, for everyone to come and celebrate. Of course, there was no charge to go to the dance; the only cost was to share your laughter and fun.

My Aunt Helen lived in our small town until the age of eighteen, and then moved to the city of Toledo, Ohio, where she attended a business college. She met the only love of her life, Jim Parker, and they were married in 1928. Things seemed to be going well for them, until the depression hit in the 1930's. Jim lost his job due to the depression, and they found they had no other choice than to move in with Jim's mother, who was already a widow, and could use the extra help. Aunt Helen says she remembers cleaning house as a full time job, usually eight to ten hours a day, and making $4.00 a week. She took care of a disabled lady, and attended to her washing, cooking, cleaning, ironing, and anything else that needed done. She and Jim continued to go to church and thank God for what they did have, instead of complaining about the things they didn't have. She says they always felt fortunate and knew that God was watching out for them. Jim came from a family of 16 children, and he too, was brought up in the Catholic faith. He knew the importance of having that faith and depending on God for everything that was important in his life. They knew that God was there, and they knew that His love and blessings would be enough to grant them the endurance to make it through this depression, and to come out to be stronger people. During this time of failed incomes and not having any extra money at all, people would get together to play cards on Saturday nights and enjoy peanut butter and lettuce sandwiches as their special edition to a pot luck supper. Those were the days when having fun were absolutely free, and there was no cost to going out and having a good time.

God saw them through the depression, just as they knew He would. They were able to get out and get an apartment of their own, they both found work again, and they continued to thank God for never letting them down. They never had any children of their own, but again, they never questioned God as to "why", they just accepted it.

Little did they know that they would be asking God to help them endure World War II, which was after they got on their feet after the depression. And once again, there He was giving them strength and hope for tomorrow, which did come later on. She says that the reason they never gave up was because they knew God was always there. I asked her if there was ever a time when they questioned His presence in those hard times, and without a second thought, she said very sharply, "No!" I admire the perserverance they had in their heart back in those days. It seems as if it would have been very easy to give up, but instead they used the hard times to help each other out, and to grow even closer in prayer to our Lord.

They survived the depression, they survived the war, and then Jim was facing health issues which would last for approximately ten years before his death. Again, instead of questioning God, they turned to Him for guidance and strength. After pneumonia, a weakened heart and liver ended up taking his life, Aunt Helen was left alone. This would end up taking her into a chapter of her life where she lived alone for more than thirty-nine years.

She has told me many times that she was so undecided of whether she should stay in Toledo where she had lived for nearly forty years, or whether she should move back to her small town of Edgerton where she had grown up and her family still was. She said she just kept praying to God that He would send her a sign that would be her answer. One weekend she came back to visit, and she noticed a small house for sale. She made an appointment to go see it, and she said she knew in her heart that she had just received God's answer. She bought the house shortly after that, and in 1970 moved back to her childhood town once again. I've asked her several times if she ever got lonely for a companion, or ever had the desire to marry again. She answered me with a reply that proved her dedication to God. She told me that God was her companion and that she never needed anyone else. How beautiful to think that someone can consider God to be her best friend and companion.

Today at the age of ninety-five, she still says that she knows God brought her back here to Edgerton to spend the rest of her life with her family. She thanks God everyday for all the blessings that He has given her. To hear her talk, you would think that she has never had a hard time in her life, but I know better. She found good out of hardship, she found peace after the war, and she found the only companion whom she ever needed, our Lord and Savior. She tells me today that she knows that her life has been really blessed, and that she feels very fortunate with what God has given to her in her life. She still lives in that same house that God showed to her in 1969 when she came back for a weekend visit. I guess that's proof enough that God was watching over her and leading her back here to spend the rest of her life.

Recently, on Holy Thursday of this year, as she was walking into church, she tripped and fell. The EMS was called to the church where they transported her to the hospital to check her out. The only thing she was worried about while lying in the emergency room was the fact that we (my husband and I and herself) were missing Mass at that same time. I told her that I knew that God would not be upset with our not being there. There she was, worrying more about missing Mass than what she was about having any broken bones or any permanent damage. I guess that only goes to show the devotion she has for our Lord. I've told her before that when she leaves this earth, her soul will reach the gates of Heaven before her heart quits beating on this earth. She doesn't believe me.

I have learned so much from her, and I hope that I can pass on her words of wisdom to another generation who will cherish the love of God in their life like she has. I pray that if I can live as long as she has that someday when someone calls me in the middle of the day to see what I'm doing, that I will answer in the same way she does now. "Oh, I'm just sitting here saying my prayers."

She came from a generation of faithful and dedicated servants of God who depended on Him for their every breath, and for their every step that they took in their lives. It is so obvious that God had her hand throughout her entire life, and that He is still guiding her this day. I pray that someday, someone may be able to look at me and see that same unending and unconditional dedicated faith in God that I see in her. If so, then my life will be as rich as what hers has been.

I wrote a poem several years ago, and now I see that it reminds me of the way that my Aunt Helen has endured her trials and how she has always came out of them with a stonger faith than before. She was always listening to what God was trying to tell her.

When Will He Answer

Don't ever get discouraged
And feel like God's not there,
He always watches over us
He is with us everywhere.

Sometimes prayers go unanswered
And we think He doesn't hear,
He wants us to be faithful
And to pray away our fear.

So when the sky is gray
And raindrops seem to fall,
Just listen for God's voice
And wait for Him to call.

For He will answer someday
If we just pray till then,
Our prayers will all be answered
Just be faithful until then.

PSALM 121:1-2

"I RAISE MY EYES TOWARDS THE MOUNTAINS, FROM WHERE WILL MY HELP COME? MY HELP COMES FROM THE LORD, THE MAKER OF HEAVEN AND EARTH."

REFLECTION:

Some people depend on God for their every need, and can truly inspire us in our lives. Do you know of someone who you can look up to, and be able to clearly see the faith that carried them through their life?

Dear Heavenly Father

It is so inspiring to witness the life of someone who has never let go of Your hand. Thank You for giving us those people in our lives. How hopeful it is to know that we, too, can share that same relationship with You. Please be with us in our lives so that we may continue to grow in Your mercy and love. Guide us on a path in which our faith will sustain us through the storms of life. Help us to be brave enough to share our faith with all others on this journey. In the most precious name of Your Son, Jesus Christ. Amen.

A Journey To Heaven

I had no idea when I wrote the chapter, "A Lifetime Of Faith", that my Aunt Helen would not live to see this book published. I thank God that He found the time for me to go down and sit with her and take notes in order to put that chapter together. I read it to her after I wrote it, and she seemed to think that I bragged on her a little too much. I think she deserved it. Four months after writing that chapter, I called her on a typical Saturday afternoon to let her know that we would be there about 6:40 p.m. that evening to pick her up for church as we always did on Saturday nights. She told me she wasn't feeling well, and that her stomach was upset and she felt she should stay home. I told Victor that she must really be sick if she was going to miss Mass.

One week later on Saturday, after a week of hospitalization, and numerous tests, they still were not for sure what was wrong with her. She seemed fairly well as my cousin Carol and her family went to visit her that Saturday morning. Aunt Helen had pulled IV's out the night before, and her arms were all red and sore. She looked at Carol and me as we stood on each side of her bed and jokingly asked us what we were going to put on her to cover her arms. I thought to myself, "Is she talking about what I think she's talking about?"

Carol and I just looked at each other, wondering how we should take that statement that just so easily had fallen from Aunt Helen's lips. I made a comment to her that when something did happen, she would be knocking on Heaven's door before her heart ever quit beating here. She looked at me as honest as ever, and replied, "Well, I don't know about that."

I told her that if she didn't make it to Heaven, no one else would either. I told her that she'd be up there with the never ending rainbows, the sun shining bright, fluffy clouds drifting by, and that the angels would be singing everywhere. I can still see the sparkle in her eyes as she pulled our hands up to her cheeks, anticipating the excitement in the thought of actually being in God's home, and she said, "Oh!" and smiled as big as ever. I knew then that she was ready to "go home".

After I visited awhile, I left and told her I'd see her sometime later. Victor and I ended up going to Mass that afternoon in Hicksville, Ohio. After I received the Body and Blood of Christ, I knelt down to pray. Instantly the tears started rolling down my face like raindrops falling from the sky. I found myself begging my Heavenly Father to let me be holding her hand as He reached for her other one. I had no idea as I prayed, that God would be answering that prayer only seven hours later. After Mass, Victor and I ate supper at a little place in Hicksville, and then came back home. Around 8:00 p.m., something told me that I needed to go back to the hospital. I know now, that it wasn't "something," but "someone."

I drove back over to the hospital, with my son Ian following me in his car. Driving over to the hospital reminded me so much of God's presence because His bright full moon seemed to light my way in the dark. It gave me hope that He was there for me, and would send me enough light to brighten up what seemed to be a dark path that night. When we arrived, Ian went in to see her first, and when he came out, I could tell by the look on his face that she was not doing well. I could feel my heart filling up with fear remembering back on the experience after Communion that afternoon. I took a deep breath, and walked into the ICU unit to see her. She was trying to sleep, but she awakened, and I told her I was there. Off and on, she would turn and say, "Mary, are you still there?" I continued to reassure her that I was still there, and would stay with her.

The main nurse was on the telephone talking to my cousin, Carol, at 1:25 a.m., because my aunt did not have the "no code" on her, and he thought he should make us aware of what that meant. I was now holding on to her, and I prayed the Our Father, the Hail Mary, and I finally was given the courage to say to her, "You can go see Jesus now, Aunt Helen, its O.K., I love you so very much."

At that moment, the angels gently took her out of my arms. I knew then that God, Aunt Helen, and I were amidst the angels who had come to guide her home. It was miraculous. I knew when I called for the nurse that they would have to come in and do everything that was needed. I remember watching them for what seemed like forever, and then I turned and walked towards the window. As I looked into the darkened night which was partially lit up from the full moon, I could clearly visualize God holding out His hands to her, and her putting her hands into His. I also could see the doctors who seemed to be trying to pull her back down. I once again prayed, "Dear God, please don't let them bring her back."

It had taken her 96 years to reach Heaven's gate, and she did everything she possibly could to get there, how could we ever take that sacred moment away from her? I left the room, and stood at the end of the nurses' station. What seemed like hours later, the medical crew walked down the hall, and said to me, "We're sorry, we did everything we could," and all I could do was smile.

I said to them, "That's O.K., she's with Jesus now, and that's where she wants to be." I knew then that God's decision and her desire to be with Him were more powerful that anything in that room. I had called my husband when they were working on her. By the time he made it to the hospital, she was already gone. My cousin Carol came too and the three of us cried together and hung on to each other as we sat in disbelief as to what had just happened. We went back in her room, and I held Aunt Helen's hand until the funeral director came. God had put that yearning in my heart to be with her, and He had sent me to the hospital to spend those last few hours with her. He had provided the full moon to shine bright in the sky, and I knew that He would wrap His arms around each one of us, as we would attempt to put our lives back together after she was gone.

The hardest part was going to my dad's Sunday morning to tell him that his big sister had been called home the night before. He had just woken up, and he sat on the edge of his bed and cried like a baby. My heart ached for his loss, for I knew the love they had for one another, and I knew how much her friendship had helped him after mom's death ten years earlier. I also was very much aware of the faith that my father and my aunt had been blessed with. I knew that somehow, throughout the heartache he would suffer because of her absence, he would survive, and God would continue to bless all of us with the strength we would need.

Her funeral was a wonderful celebration of her ninety-six years here on earth. I could feel her presence as I held her handkerchief in my hand and read a tribute which I had written for her. As I finished reading and walked gently down the steps off the altar, I touched her casket and quietly said, "Thank you." The tears poured down my face, but it was my own selfishness that made me sad. As we played the song "I Can Only Imagine" by Mercy Me, I could just picture her dancing around with the angels in heaven. That thought surpassed any thought of her being here with us now. Her life was dedicated to God, and now He had rewarded her with an eternal life in Heaven. Her memory would continue to live on within our hearts forever.

Within the next few months, I would learn so much more about my aunt than I had ever known before. Carol and I were in charge of getting her house around for sale, and we had decided we would have an estate sale in the house of her personal belongings before the sale of the house. I inherited her dining room table, her china cabinet, and a bedroom set that belonged to my grandparents' years ago. Going through all of her belongings brought about a sense of peace, because I learned even more about her relationship with God. I think she had saved every holy card she had ever received, and little inspirational prayers were found in about every corner of the house. Throughout the time we were getting ready for the sale, we could feel her presence everywhere. I would pick up an item and say to Carol, "How much should we put on this?" No matter what the item was, her estimate was within a dollar of mine. It got to the point of being funny, as we would laugh and comment on how much Aunt Helen was helping with the sale. There was never a doubt in my mind through the next few months that she was watching our every step from her new home above, and asking God to help guide us. Carol and I bonded in a way we never had, and I would have never made it through those days without her.

The day of her house sale was a dreary day that was cloudy and cold. It was in December, but no snow had fallen, and we were thankful for that. The man who ended up buying it, I heard later, had made a spur of the moment decision in his purchase. Within minutes after the sale, my husband opened up the back door and said to me, "Well I guess your Aunt Helen is pleased with the sale." I looked out to see the sun shining brighter then ever. I knew then, that she had attended the sale also, just in a different sense than we had.

I now drive past her house, and I know someone else is living there. I also know the memories that we shared in that house, and the loving meals she cooked for all of us will never be far from my heart. There was so much laughter and love shared, along with many happy birthdays celebrated, and so much fun that took place there, that it will always be "my Aunt Helen's house," no matter who lives there. I also know that throughout the months of preparing for the sale, I must have said a hundred times, "Wouldn't that be awesome if someone moved in that would let me come down for coffee now and then?" I found out last week at work that a girl that I work with had moved in, and she told me that when she got all settled, she would have me down for coffee. I guess Aunt Helen is still taking care of things. How can I ever doubt how faithful our Lord is?

Through her death, I learned so many things. She had helped us with the sale of her belongings and the sale of the house. She had passed her unending faith down to us through the laughter and tears that we shared together after her death. I also knew that because of her, someday this book would get finished and would be published. God was there through it all, walking with us every step we took.

I have experienced a real peace knowing that I will truly see her again someday, if I can only live my life as close to our Lord as what she did. Her memory will live on every day, and I will always hear that cute little chuckle of hers every time I start to miss her. At the top of her funeral card, I wrote a short little poem which consisted of four lines. Later on, I would realize how much more could be added about the night she went home.

My Journey To Heaven

I waited for many many years
For God to call me home.
His full moon seemed to light the sky
When the angels brought me home.

My new life has just begun
In God's beautiful home above,
I've never felt this peace before
Or been surrounded by so much love.

I know you must be sad right now
But please don't cry for me,
I'm in the arms of Jesus
And my spirit has been set free.

Someday I'll stand at Heaven's gate
And I'll be waiting just for you,
We'll be reunited for eternity
In God's peaceful sky so blue.

I know that death is not the end, but a beautiful new beginning of a life that God has promised to all who believe. I will never forget the excited look on Aunt Helen's face as I mentioned eternity with Jesus. That alone will bring me comfort whenever I start to miss her. That alone will give me hope in every sunrise that I witness from now on.

LUKE 6:23

"REJOICE AND LEAP FOR JOY ON THAT DAY! BEHOLD, YOUR REWARD WILL BE GREAT IN HEAVEN."

REFLECTION:

We should live our lives with only one goal in mind, and that is to get to Heaven. If this was your last day on earth, would you be confident that you would spend eternity with God in His Heavenly Kingdom?

Dear Heavenly Father

It is a blessing to be able to hold someone's hand, as You are reaching for their other one to take them home to Your Kingdom. Thank You for such a wonderful experience. Help us to live our lives obeying Your commandments, so that we too, may be reunited someday with You in Heaven. I use to be so frightened of death, but experiencing this with others, and being able to feel the presence of the angels, has made me realize that it is only a new beginning of eternity with You. Help us to know that death has no end for those who love You. In the most precious name of Your Son, Jesus Christ. Amen.

Another Goodbye

I remember well the day I wrote the chapter, "My Father's Love." It was a warm day in June, and when I finished it, I went right down to my dad's so I could read it to him. I can still see the tears in his eyes as I thanked him for being the kind of father that he was, and for praising God for all that He had done to find me the perfect father. I can still feel the warmth of his arms around me as I got ready to leave after I had read it, and we had visited awhile. Looking back now, I am so thankful that I shared it with him that day nearly two years ago, because he too, would be going home to see his Heavenly Father before this book would ever be finished. I feel in my heart that God allowed me the opportunity to share with my dear Aunt Helen and my dear father the parts of this book which would certainly bring joy to their hearts.

My dad had Parkinson's disease, and although he handled it very well, last summer on a Sunday morning when he did not answer his phone, I knew something was wrong. I sent my husband over to check on him, and he found him on the floor of his bedroom not able to get up. He spent three days in the hospital, and then to his disapproval, ended up going to a nursing center for rehabilitation. He was not at all happy about it, but I worked full time and there was no one to be able to take care of him. For the first two weeks, everytime I left there, I would cry for hours.

I felt like I was neglecting him, even if I was there everyday at least twice. He was so homesick for his modest little trailer that he and mom had shared for over thirty years, and nothing I could say seemed to take that yearning away. Little by little, he started joking around with all the nurses and aids, and he seemed to start getting back to his ornery old self. He gained weight, played lots of cards and bingo, and actually started to make himself at home. I started to leave there everyday with a lighter heart and a smile on my face. It was good to see him happy again. I don't think he ever gave up on the idea of going home until one day I took him there on a Sunday afternoon. It was a real job getting him up the steps by myself, and into the trailer. As he sadly looked around the living room, he said very softly, "Honey, I don't think I'll ever be able to come back here by myself." He said it with hesitation, but also with acceptance. I felt better after that day, and knew that God had arranged that afternoon for a specific reason. Dad realized that his life in the trailer was over, and that he had to make the best of his new home, and I, in return, left there no longer saddened by the fact that he did not have his own home to come home too. It was an afternoon of acceptance, and we both needed it.

Over the next five months seemed to be up and down for him. Some days he felt really good, and seemed to be stronger, and then other days, he didn't seem to do as good. I was called out of work one cold November day, because he had been taken to the hospital by EMS. The next nine days would be the final days of his life here on earth. In my heart, I knew his days had become numbered, although that is one of the hardest things to have to face. I still missed my mother terribly, and then to think of facing life without either parent was something I didn't want to think about. After spending four days in the hospital, he was released to go back to the nursing home.

From that day on, I was on a family medical leave from work, and I stayed at the nursing center every day and night with him, except to go home each night for about an hour to shower and collect my thoughts. I prayed daily that I would be able to be with my father when he took his last breath on earth. He had been there for me my whole life, and I wanted to be there for him. No one knows what someone is going through as they die, but I wanted to reassure him that he would not be alone. I was sitting in his recliner beside his bed probably three or four days before he died, and I was writing something. His head came off the pillow, and he looked at me and asked,"Honey, are you working on your book?"

I replied. "No, should I be?"

He very sternly said "Yes!" From that moment on I knew that I needed to start working on getting this book published. During the time that he had been taken to the hospital, I had also found out that my job of nearly twenty-two years would be closing their doors at the end of the year. I had lots of goodbyes ahead of me in the next month which I did not want to have to say.

Those last nine days of his life meant so much to me to be able to share them with him, to hold his hand, to read Psalms out of the Bible when he was restless, to sit at his bedside and pray a rosary for him asking God to bless him with the strength and courage he needed. I would not trade those days for anything in the world. One of the aids came up to me a few days before he died, and shared with me that he had told her the night before that he had saw an angel. I told her I didn't doubt it a bit, and that I was happy that she had felt the need to tell me that. She said sometimes, she never knows how a family will react when it comes to situations like that, but she felt she needed to tell me. That was the sign I needed that I knew he was going to be alright. The only thing I wondered then was if it was my mother that he had seen. After all, they say when a person gets close to death, they see the other side, and sometimes reach for it. He was reaching too, for I knew he saw many beautiful things. I had started writing my dad a letter as I sat in his trailer a few months before all this, and I wrote off and on after that. It ended up being the tribute that I would read at this funeral. It ended up being the final words of thanksgiving to him that I could offer. People asked me how I ever got up at his funeral and read it all, but I told them I had plenty of help. I knew how much I loved my dad, and how much he loved me, and I think when there's that much love, that anything is possible.

I could physically feel his presence within my heart as I stood in the church and proudly read my final thank you to him. When the tears started to fall, I would look at his picture in front of me, and I would take a deep breath and start again. It was as if he was on one side of me, and Christ was on the other side holding me up. I never faltered, I just kept going.

After I was finished reading, we played Bette Middler's "Wind Beneath My Wings". We had used the same song at mom's funeral eleven years before. My daughter Christie had suggested we use it this time also. I wasn't sure that was the song we were supposed to use. The decision was made simple when I got out a photo album that I had made for dad years earlier. As I opened it, the first thing I saw was my handwritten message, "Dad, my hero." Part of the lyrics to that song is, "Did I ever tell you you're my hero?" It was perfect for both of them, because they had both been my heroes in my life. I want to share my letter to my dad with you so that you may clearly understand my life, and where my faith had so easily come from. This is the letter in its entirety that I read at his funeral.

Friday, Oct. 30, 2004

Dear Dad,

As I sit here in the quietness of your trailer, with the full moon shining in the window, my mind wanders back to the time when you and mom sat in these very same chairs. Right now, that seems so very long ago, but yet I can still smell cigar aroma lingering in the air, I can still hear laughter filling the room, a game on the TV playing, and I can truly feel the presence of God, and the love for family tucked inside of the walls of this humble little trailer. I look around and I don't see expensive pictures hanging on the walls, instead there are four crucifixes hanging in this living room alone. There is Mother and Dad plaques telling the kind of parents you have been. There are family pictures bringing back memories of wonderful and happy times of the past, and also pictures which hold no memory for me because of their age, but which gives me a sense of how important "family" was to both of you. As I sit here in the stillness, I can honestly say without a doubt that "Christ was the head of this house, the unseen guest at every meal, and the silent listener to every conversation." You and mom not only invited Him into your home, you allowed Him to be present deep within your hearts every single day of your lives, no matter where you lived. I can still remember the same peaceful loving feeling as we grew up on the farm, witnessing God's beautiful sunrise every morning, and seeing the majestic beauty of His sunset every evening over the field of corn across the road. Steve and I have been so very fortunate, and so very blessed that God chose you and mom out of everyone He created to become our parents. Had He not, maybe I wouldn't know of His love like I do now. That faithful and unending, unconditional love that a father has for his children. I guess that's why it's been so easy to accept God's love, because your love for Steve and I has been as great as God's love for all of His children. You have reminded me over and over again that while you were growing up your father would always say to you, "Don't ever give up your faith, son, don't ever give up your faith." You told me to never forget that no matter what happened in my life. You and mom always said that there was a reason for everything, no matter how hopeless it looked at the time. You have truly helped me to believe that. I know that the strong faith that you and mom handed down, will be the glue that keeps life together at times when it would be so easy to fall apart.

That faith of yours was just as strong when we were growing up. Going to church on Sunday mornings, and other times, was as ordinary as getting up each day. Praying before every meal, always giving thanks for what we had, instead of questioning what we didn't have. Always depending on God for everything you ever needed, made us realize what the important things were. Riches and material things were not what you and mom asked for. It was God's blessing over your family and His guidance everyday that you prayed for. It was His love and faithfulness that you depended on.

You have been such a remarkable father, from taking time to play ball with us and the neighbors in the country while growing up, to hopping off the tractor to go to one of my drillteam parades, or a ballgame of Steve's. You were always there for us, trying to guide us in the right direction. I don't know if we were always listening like we should, but you were always there, trying to give us good advice so our lives would be complete and happy.

Besides being a perfect father, you were a perfect husband too. The only time I remember mom getting mad at you was when you were twirling a basketball on your finger to show Steve how it was done, (I still think you were showing off), but somehow it fell and landed in Steve's birthday cake that Mom had just finished decorating. I can still hear her saying in a voice louder than she had ever spoke, "Hinie Cape"! I guess that's not a bad record for a wife to get mad at a husband only once. In fact, I don't even think it's normal. You and mom had a very unique relationship. God brought you and mom together in June, and united you in marriage only seven months later in January. That is true love that has been blessed by God. That faithful strong love remained in your marriage for nearly forty five years until mom went home to be with Our Lord. During the last three years of her life, which was spent in the nursing home, you were there each and every day, at least twice. I don't remember you missing a day unless you were sick. You were so dedicated to her, and showed her so much love. It has been a blessing to have parents who were so faithful to each other.I'll bet the only time you ever neglected her would have been for an athletic event. Imagine that! I really don't think that she ever felt neglected; I think that she, along with many others, was fascinated by your love for sports.

All of your grandchildren will remember sitting on your lap while you told them crazy stories, and shared many many jokes with them, and little sayings that will long be remembered. You were such a fun grandpa, and they loved you very much.

I have never met a man who was more loving, humorous, and sociable than you. I remember some of your old joking around like, "That's not the same girl you had with you last night, is it?" While cleaning out some of the things in your trailer, I found a picture of your 25th wedding anniversary in the newspaper, and below it was that same saying handwritten. Another newspaper picture I found was the one where you were standing, with arm outstretched and finger pointed. It must have been that one and only time when you were yelling at a referee. Someone wrote above the picture, "Down in front." I wonder now if you ever found out who sent you those. I don't know how many times people have reminded me that their fond memory of you at games was when you would pull out your wallet, and ask a referee, ""How much is it going to take?" Some of your other crazy sayings like, "For cracking ice, holy Toledo." And then when you would tell other people that you could speak five different languages. They would look at you wondering if you really could, no one ever knew whether to take you serious or not. I guess that's what made you so much fun, because you always kept everyone on their toes. "Mama Mia" , "Hash ca mash ca baby", "Abiel Stestack", "What's your name, puddin tame" ,"See you later alligator, after while crocodile" are only a few of the many sayings that you said over and over, and will always bring a smile to our face when we remember them. I don't think any of us ever knew what they meant though. The laughter in your heart you shared with everyone who ever knew you.

Mon. Nov. 8, 2004

Yesterday, before you were released from the hospital, you looked at me sadly and said, "I don't know if I will make it to the first basketball games or not." I told you that if you didn't have a front row seat here, you would have one up there, so either way you would be at those games." It has been exactly eleven years ago today that God sent His angels to take Mom home. Watching you today at the nursing home, I can see how very tired you are. I have told myself over and over again, that when God sends His angels for you, that it will be the happiest day of your life. It will be a reunion with mom, and the rest of your family. The only other day that maybe could compare would be the 1959 State Basketball Championship when your Edgerton Bulldogs won!!!! O.K., I know you were pretty happy the days which you brought Steve and I home from Cleveland, too.

I do know that you have lived your entire life as a hard working, honest, loving and caring man who loved the Lord with all his heart. Your reward will be great! I can already picture you and mom dancing up in Heaven to Lawrence Welk's music played by a choir of angels.

Tues. Nov. 16, 2004

It is 4:55 a.m. As I sit here holding your hand, I know your new life in the Heavenly kingdom will begin soon. You have no idea how many tears will be shed over your leaving, how many smiles will appear when remembering the happy times, the laughter that will be shared bringing back all the crazy jokes you use to tell, and your sayings that will probably live on forever. Last night, when second shift was leaving here at the nursing home, some of "your girls" came in to give you a kiss and to say what was on their hearts. We gathered hand in hand around the foot of your bed, and prayed the Lord's Prayer. I felt so much love and respect going out to you in that circle of friendship. Girls who had only met you exactly five months ago today, but yet you had already touched the very depth of their hearts. I guess what you and mom said about everything happening for a reason was true. Five months ago when I brought you out here, I cried and cried because I didn't know if you would want to be here. Now I know it was God who was giving you five beautiful months of good care, girls who truly loved you, and people to play cards with. You said right up to the end, "You girls are so wonderful." It ended up being such a blessing. I prayed last night that someday you would be able to truly see all the people who loved and admired you over the years when you weren't even aware of it. I always told you that you'd better never leave this earth in the cold of the snowy winter, or the dead heat of the summer, because of the number of people who would be standing in line just to say goodbye. You used to laugh and say there wouldn't be anyone coming to see an old man like you. Well dad, I'm sure this will be one time, and probably the only time, that I will be right and you'll be wrong. You are truly a hero to me, Steve, and all of your family, and hundreds of your friends who have grown to love you so deeply over the years. I would doubt if you have any enemies anywhere. O.K., maybe a referee here or there. But I know that you have more friends than a field has dandelions on a beautiful spring day. That was so obvious when the girls' basketball team came to visit you here this week. You could not believe that they came, because you really can't understand how many people truly love you.

Wed. Nov. 17, 2004

Yesterday morning, with your children at your side, the angels came. You went peacefully, because of all the prayers that had been prayed for you. I held your hand as I released your spirit into the hands of our Heavenly Father. It was so hard to let go, but I knew of the eternal happiness that awaited you. Last night, instead of sleeping in the bed next to you, I slept in my own bed at home. After nine nights of listening to your every breath, I finally went to sleep knowing that you were alright. Victor told me today that he heard me whisper in the middle of the night, "I love you daddy, I love you daddy!"

Whenever we see the sun shining in the beautiful sky, we will remember how you warmed our hearts, the thunder will remind us of your hearty laughter, and the rainbow will help us to remember what your life meant to so many people, a beautiful and colorful life which truly believed that God had always kept his promise to be there. You will be cherished deep within our hearts for all eternity, and we will miss you more than words can say. Because of our faith, we can be reassured that we will see you again someday. When we reach the gates of Heaven and ask you how you've been, you will probably say, "Two in a row, and three in a hill". We love you, Hinie Cape, and we will never forget you.

His funeral was November 19, 2005, and it was a beautiful celebration of his life, and his love for God. He was probably the biggest fan of "The Edgerton Bulldogs" that this small town had ever known, and it was obvious at the funeral home. The high school boys' and girls' basketball teams both came to pay their respect, and to give in dad's name, a basketball award that will be given out every year to a dedicated player on that team. There was a huge "bulldog" on top of his casket, instead of the usual flower cascade. He would have been so honored. The funeral home itself looked like a "bulldog shrine", and it made me realize even more how much he was truly loved and respected. His name will live on forever through the athletic association of our small town high school, and his laughter will live on forever in the hearts of all of those he touched. On his funeral card at the top I had written a four line poem which said it all:

> *Don't cry for me, I'm finally free*
> *I'm home where I belong,*
> *I have a seat, in the front row*
> *To every game in town.*

He has a front row alright, and I know that while I am sitting here at this computer trying to get this book finished, I am sure that he is standing at the gates of Heaven watching me, and guiding me on this path. I'll bet my mom is on one side of him, and my Aunt Helen is on the other. I can feel their love pouring from the sunshine outside, and it is truly warming my heart. I can only pray that if my life on this earth can touch only a handful as many lives as my father touched in his lifetime, then my life will have accomplished my Heavenly Father's plans for me.

A few days before my dad died, I stood at the side of his bed, and I told him that mom was waiting on him to come and dance with her again. (I can remember when I was little they would dance in the living room to Lawrence Welk's show). I cried as I held his hand and gave him "permission" to go, but I knew that it was something that I had to do. I also asked him if he could talk to Jesus and ask Him if He would send me the wisdom I needed to finish this book, and get it out to inspire other people. Saying "goodbye" to someone whom you love so much is so very hard, but it is comforting to know that the person, who loved you here, is watching over you from God's Heavenly Kingdom above, and still sending you their love.

One month and one day from the day I buried my dad, I said "goodbye" to the people whom I had worked with for nearly twenty two years. Again, it was very hard to do, but I had no choice. Sometimes the word "goodbye" is inevitable, but it doesn't make it any easier. I learned a lot in those few short weeks of saying goodbye. I had no control over the closing of my factory, I had no control over my father's life on earth coming to an end, but what I did have control over was how it would affect me. I could go to pieces, and resent every goodbye that I had to say, or I could depend on God for strength and courage to face the uncertain days ahead, and be thankful that I had the relationships for as long as I did. I chose to depend on God, and as always, He took my hand and walked with me on that lonely path. It wasn't an easy winter, but I made it! Thank God again for the gift of my faith, which allows me to say "goodbye" but to carry the memories in my heart that will last a lifetime.

"THE LORD IS MY STRENGTH AND MY SHIELD, IN WHOM MY HEART TRUSTED AND FOUND HELP. SO MY HEART REJOICES; WITH MY SONG I PRAISE MY GOD."

REFLECTION:

We have probably all had to say goodbye to someone we loved, or knew of someone who had lost a loved one. Did you ask God for His healing hand upon your saddened heart, and trust in Him for strength for the next day, and pass that hope on to others?

Dear Heavenly Father

It is so hard to say goodbye to those we love. Thank You for being there in our time of need. It is comforting to know that when someone is being called home, we are sometimes given the chance to be with them so they do not feel alone. Give us courage to spend time with those whose days on earth are close to an end. Help us to be able to pray the comforting words that You know they need to hear. We know we can count on You to send us to those who need us. In the most precious name of Your Son, Jesus Christ. Amen.

When God Speaks

This morning while drinking my coffee, I sat and started crying because sometimes I feel so overwhelmed I don't know what to do. It has now been four months since my factory closed, and as I started thinking about all the things I have not gotten done since that day, it seemed like I lost sight of everything that God had helped me to accomplish. I sat at the kitchen table looking out at the sun shining across my back yard, but instead of focusing on the beautiful sun, I noticed the smears on my windows and dirt on the screens. The sun shining across the kitchen floor made it even more obvious of the dust that was accumulating and the dust particles that were just floating around in the air. I began to feel very negative about my time off work.

I remember when I used to think that if I ever had any time off, my house would be spotless. Now I was not working and I have not felt like I had accomplished anything worthwhile. I was mentally beating myself up when the phone rang. The caller ID showed me that it was my daughter Christie. It scared me when I saw her name, because she never calls me that early in the morning. As soon as I heard her voice, I cried even harder. Christie and I have always been very close and been able to read through all the "everything is fine" line. When she asked what I was doing, all I could do was cry. I started explaining to her what I was thinking. She reminded me that it had only been five months ago when my dad had passed away, and that it had been a long and cold winter, with a lot of emotional stress to endure. She told me it was O.K. if I had not done any major house cleaning and that I had needed some time to rest and relax.

Losing my aunt in October of 2003, my dad in November of 2004, and then the closing of my factory in December 2004 had definitely been a lot to endure. Some days I feel like I just can't comprehend anything at all, and I lose my focus so easily. Christie reassured me that it was O.K. to feel like that, and that I needed to stop feeling so bad about things I haven't done and to look at the things I have done. There is only one thing worse than your child not listening to you. It is when they grow up to be an adult and they are giving "your" advice back to you because they learned it from you years ago. When she started giving me my pep talk, I said "O.K., O.K.," but she continued to show me the things that she respected me for that I was not even aware of.

A lot of things had happened in these last few months which I was very much aware of, but not looking it at in the sense that she was. We talked for over an hour on the phone, and by the time she lifted my spirits and my five year old grandson told me "knock knock jokes," I was in a lot better frame of mind when I hung up.

I ask the Lord what I should do today, and when I picked up my "One Bread, One Body" daily devotional and read today's message, I knew what I should do today. The "praise" for today quoted, "St. Mark spread the gospel far beyond his homeland and people by obeying the promptings of the Holy Spirit and writing it down for countless others to read." Today I will share with you all the things that my daughter reminded me that I have done over the past few months, instead of worrying about all the things I think I haven't done. I will share with you what God has been so busy at these days.

Since I have been off work, I have had the opportunity to go to church almost daily for some type of church service. Certain days there is Mass, and other days there is Communion Service. It has been a wonderful way to start the day in the presence of the Lord in His home. I still think there is something real special about just being in His house and sitting quietly to see what He will say to me. I have heard Him speak a lot since I have had more quiet time to listen to Him.

A few weeks ago, after receiving the Body of Christ, I knelt in silence to absorb His presence within me. I felt very strongly about a girl whose husband had just joined our church this Easter and wanted to invite her to come and pray a rosary with me someday. I could picture us kneeling in the front row where I usually go when I am by myself and spend time with the Lord. I had a lot of mixed feelings about inviting her, because I had heard that she was unsure of her husband's decision to join the church. The feeling grew as I continued to question the purpose of this nudging that I was receiving. Sometimes it is so hard to react when we have to step out of our comfort zone, but yet, the feeling was not leaving. I knew the Lord was calling me to do this, and I knew that I wanted to obey Him, even if I did feel a little strange doing it.

I did call her that day and explained my intentions. I remember telling her that I hoped she didn't think I was crazy. I told her exactly what I heard the Lord telling me to do. She said she didn't think I was crazy, and she agreed to go. That rosary that we prayed together ended up bringing her to ask many questions about my faith. She had been attending church with her husband since he had attended a Christ Renews His Parish weekend earlier in the year. Now she was starting to "feel" the excitement that her husband had been experiencing for quite some time. She comes to church a lot with me now, embracing her yearning for becoming closer to God. I feel like my own faith has been deepened from trying to answer her questions and having to look at my own spiritual life which sometimes seems to have a lot of room for growth. The strangest thing about this whole story is that we had known each other for quite some time. Not very well, but we had spoken at different times before. It is all different now because God has brought us together for a reason, and although neither one of us may know what it is for right now, we are both excited to see where He is taking us. I just know I am happy that I heard God calling me to do that and that I listened to Him.

Another time I heard God speak to me was in church one day when I was there for Adoration. Sitting alone with our Lord in the silence of His home gives me a real sense of His presence. In the stillness there is a peace which seems to take over the entire body. It is a peace which leaves you wondering how one ever gets through life without God's love. I had started taking a notepad with me when I went to Adoration just in case God gave me some insights as to my life and my experiences with Him. This poem came to me one day as I sat in that same front row looking upon Jesus hanging on that cross. It was a real revelation of my life and how the struggles had become my treasures to embrace with faith.

Oh Dear Jesus

I look back on the times in my life
When I struggled and I fell,
Sometimes I didn't know You were there
I don't know why I couldn't tell.

There were times of tears and loneliness
When I felt so much alone,
There were times I would cry out to You
And wait in silence all alone.

So many times I could not hear
You answering my call,
I wondered if You loved me
Or if You even cared at all.

But I'd look up at the darkened sky
And I'd see a million stars,
I knew that You had to be there
Sometimes You just seemed so afar.

I know now that You watched over me
With Your tender and loving care,
I know now that You were with me
Even when I couldn't feel You there.

How can I ever thank You enough
For all that You have done,
What can I do to give You my love
For this heart that You have won.

I want to be fully open to You
And to never let You down,
I want to help all others believe
That You are always around.

Please help me live my life for You
And to share Your forgiveness and love,
Please shower me with Your strength and peace
From Your Heavenly Kingdom above.

You know who needs You desperately
Please send them to my heart,
Please give me all the tools I need
To help them make a new start.

I know now why the struggles came
And tears would easily fall,
I know now why sometimes I felt
You could not hear my call.

For it was in those darkest times
I needed You so very much,
It was times when my heart was broken
That I would call for Your gentle touch.

Those storms in life taught me patience
And compassion came from the tears,
The times I felt so all alone
Helped me find courage to face my fears.

So now that I look back on my life
I can feel so very blessed,
My love for You has truly grown
From the pain of trials and tests.

If my life had gone so perfectly
Would my heart yearn just for You,
If I had never cried before
Would I know that You're faithful and true?

Dear Jesus, I want to share Your love
With others everyday
Please help me on this journey
Please light and guide my way.

This love that burns deep in my heart
I want others to feel it too,
Oh Lord, I praise You so very much
For everything that You do.

My heart is truly open to You
Let me know Your will for me,
My life is truly in Your hands
Open my eyes so they may see.

I thank You for my tears and trials
And Your sunshine that brightens this land,
I thank You for always loving me
And for never letting go of my hand.

That night in prayer group I pulled out that notepad, and a friend jokingly said to me, "Which chapter is this?" At the time, I had no idea that it would be in this book someday. I guess this shows that no matter what happens in our lives, God is in control, and He will continue to be. As I read it that night in church, I knew that other people could look back on their own lives and recognize the times when they, too, felt alone. Now they can rejoice because of their spiritual growth during those times.

The next morning when I went to Communion service, we prayed a rosary afterwards. As I knelt before the Christ Child on the side altar, I once again, felt this urge to leave my comfort zone. It was a need to go home and call "Cindy", and read her the poem I had written the day before. Cindy and I had also gotten acquainted through Christ Renews His Parish a few years before. We keep in touch once in awhile, but not on a regular basis by any means. As I walked into my house, I knew that I had to call her. In the back of my mind, I was asking the Lord, "What am I supposed to say to her?" Again, He told me just to call her and read it to her. So I dialed her number, and her daughter answered and told me she had just left for work and that I could call her there. It was something I had never done before, although she had given me her work number at one time in case I ever needed to get ahold of her. So I called her and said, "I wrote a poem yesterday in church, and I have a strong feeling that I am suppose to read it to you. I hope you don't think I'm crazy," I said with a chuckle.

She never questioned me, she just said, "O.K." I read it to her, and we talked for a few minutes, and then we hung up. I wondered after I hung up the phone exactly what went through her mind when I called, but I knew that the Lord must have had His reasons. I laughed to myself as I questioned whether I would ever know or not. The next morning, I received a call from our prayer chain at St. Mary's that her nineteen month old grandson had been admitted to the hospital with pneumonia. I thought it was kind of strange that she had not said anything the day before when I called her. In fact I started feeling rather guilty for possibly rambling on and maybe not giving her a chance to tell me. Sometimes when I start talking, it's hard to get a word in. I was pretty busy the rest of the day, and didn't ponder on it anymore.

That night after Victor and I got home from Mass and had just settled in, the phone rang. It was Cindy. She sounded pretty serious as she said, "I know why you were supposed to call me yesterday and read that poem to me. Forty-five minutes after I hung up talking to you, I received a phone call telling me my grandson was in the hospital. I knew immediately that God was handling everything, and that my grandson was going to be alright. I knew that He was not going to let go of my hand through this, and that I had nothing to worry about."

She told me that while she was driving home from the hospital that night, everything from the day before became a clear picture. I had called her and read her a poem that I had just written the day before not even understanding why. The words of the poem helped her to realize when she got her phone call that things would be alright. I had asked God in my prayer to send me the people who needed Him, and He had.

Was it all in God's plan? I certainly believe that He does know what each one of us needs. He picks out someone to deliver the message whom we least expect, and then He sits back and waits to see if we will be obedient. It is an absolute incredible feeling when you find out the Lord is using you in such remarkable ways. I had written a request to Him to use me, and He had, and I was ever so grateful. The very next week at Children's Mass Father Tom spoke to the children about listening for God to speak to them. He told them if they obeyed God, He would trust them with more. I felt like a child all over again, with all that excitement that I had done what God wanted me to do. The reward was great. As I sat there listening to Father's words, the smile in my heart could not have been erased. I knew exactly what he was talking about, and I knew that everyone of those children would know someday too, if they don't already.

Listening to God speaking to us is so much fun. His timing is so perfect, just like the moment when my daughter called me this morning. When we feel these nudges that He's giving us something to do, or when we quietly "hear" Him asking us to do something, we can be very thankful that He trusts us enough to do His work. After all, His work is very special. He has chosen each one of us to touch someone's heart. Whose heart do you think He's asking you to touch today? If you listen, and ask Him to show you, He will answer if you are truly open to His will.

After my dad died last fall, one of my friends sent a long stem rose, and a little rock that said, "When God closes a door He opens another." I feel like that is what happened after my factory closed. Before there were so many times I wanted to just sit down and write the thoughts that were heavily on my mind, but I couldn't seem to find the time. Now I have extra time to go to His home, and just quietly listen for His response. It has been a time of reflection and meditation. The quiet time I spend with Him now fills me with hope. It seems as though there were so many signs out there and now all of a sudden, I can see them in a way so much more obvious than ever before.

This last winter as I prepared to move my dad's trailer into another park, I cried everytime I went down there to work. Sometimes I would miss dad and mom so much that I would just sit in his chair and feel sorry for myself because I didn't have them anymore. One day in particular, on the Friday before they were going to move the trailer the next week, I loaded up some boxes of pictures and personal things to take to my house until I could figure out what to do with everything. I was crying when I left his trailer. When I got uptown, I was sitting at the stop light remembering that I had told my friend Chris at prayer group the night before, that I would stop in to see her at the restaurant where she worked. I was in no mood to stop and chat with tears streaming down my face. I thought to myself that if there was a parking place in front of the restaurant, that I would run in for just a minute and say "Hi" to her. There is never an empty parking place that time of day, so I knew I was safe. When I went a block further, there was the empty place right in front of the door. I knew then that I had to stop and go inside.

As I walked through the restaurant, Chris saw me walking towards her and came up and hugged me. She asked me what I was doing. Immediately I started crying even harder. She looked at me and asked me what was wrong. I told her about my morning and my tasks that I did not want to do. All of a sudden, I heard the song "Wind Beneath My Wings" in the background. I asked her if she heard something, but it was obvious that I was the only one who could hear it. I asked her if she had a radio on, and she said there was one over in the corner. She walked over and turned it up only to hear the song that I had been hearing seconds before. Tears really started running down my cheeks, remembering back on playing that song in tribute to my mother at her funeral eleven years before that, and also at dad's funeral only five months earlier.

I started laughing at the same time that I was crying. It was as though they were both watching over me to tell me that everything I was doing was the right thing, and that everything was going to be alright. It was as if they were saying to me that they were with me through it all. What if I had left dad's trailer two minutes earlier or two minutes later? What if there had not been a parking space there in front? What if I had not stopped to say hi to my friend? It really doesn't matter because everything happened the way it was supposed to. I believe that God knew that I needed a reassurance that I was doing a good job, and that everything would turn out alright. I received my message and the rest of the day went better than I ever expected.

There are times when I get so caught up in the trials of life that it is easy to lose sight of everything. Then all of a sudden when we least expect it, God sends us a message of hope and encouragement. If we're too busy being occupied with everything else, it is easy to not even hear what He's trying to tell us.

Everyday is a new day. Everyday is a brand new opportunity to open ourselves to a new assignment given by God. I've decided my daughter was right. If I would have been washing my smudgy windows instead of listening to God calling me to minister to someone, then I would have missed His blessing. If I would not have asked Him to send someone to me that needed Him, then I wouldn't have had the chance to share His love with another child of His.

I obeyed Him and did what I felt He was calling me to do. He blessed me abundantly in return.

I don't ever want to miss another opportunity to share with someone what I have learned of His love. I want to accomplish everything that He has planned for me to do. The next time I look out to see the sun coming up, I will ask myself who I can share His warmth with, instead of seeing windows that need cleaning.

PSALM 40:9

"TO DO YOUR WILL IS MY DELIGHT; MY GOD, YOUR LAW IS IN MY HEART."

REFLECTION:

God speaks to us in many different ways. Is God asking you today to touch someone's heart, or give someone a message from Him? If you hear Him speak to you, are you going to be obedient, and accept His blessings that will follow?

Dear Heavenly Father

Thank You for letting us hear Your voice, and for asking us to do things for You. It is such an honor to be able to bring people closer to You, and to help our own hearts grow into an even deeper relationship with You. Please open our ears, hearts, and minds, so that we may be open to whatever You need us to do. Fill those hearts with peace in knowing that it is truly You whom they hear. In the most precious name of Your Son, Jesus Christ. Amen.

The End Of The Rainbow

Whenever we see a rainbow in the sky, we know that we will always see another one someday. I have been inspired by rainbows my whole life. As a child, I could just picture my Heavenly Father in Heaven using paint brushes to decorate the sky. I just couldn't figure out how He could get from one side of the sky to the other in just a matter of minutes. I guess that's called the miracle of God. As I learned about the flood in Genesis, and how God sent His rainbow as a covenant that He would never again flood the earth and destroy it, I was reminded of what I should think of everytime I see His rainbow painted across the beautiful blue sky.

As a child growing up in the country, I could see for miles and miles, and I often wondered how one could ever possibly find the end of the rainbow. I wondered if I just started walking one day across the fields of corn, if I would eventually find it. Of course, when you are a child growing up, you are sure that there is a pot of gold at the end of the rainbow, which would make it even more exciting to find.

I did a lot of walking out in the country when I was a child, but never did find the end of the rainbow or the pot of gold. I think it was because God wanted me to discover them later on in my life. As I finish writing this book, I realize that I have found them. I have learned that if you have God in your life, and have family and friends who love Him as you do, then you have found pure gold within your heart and soul. The world in which my parents raised me, inspired me to believe that finding the end of the rainbow is simply walking the journey from a heart filled with love to a soul filled with faith.

It has taken many years to walk this journey. During the miles of looking for the end of the rainbow, I cried many tears, and my heart held much sadness at times. I also laughed a lot, and then my heart was filled with as much joy as what it could possibly hold. But God never let go of my hand, and He never let me quit thinking about this dream. As I said before, it was my mother's dream for me to write a book, and then when God took her home, it became my dream.

I realize now that God was having my mother prepare me for what He had planned for my life. I just didn't know it at the time. Maybe she didn't know it either, but I know that she listened to what God was telling her to tell me. She obeyed Him, and she never quit instilling that dream in me, even up to her dying days. When she went home to be with God, my dear Aunt Helen and my dad continued to remind me of that same vision. I think when mom made it to Heaven, she must have told God that sometimes I didn't listen well, and that I would have to keep getting reassurances of His will for me. Between my Aunt Helen and my dad, it was mentioned several times. They would get so excited when I would tell them of my ideas for the book. They kept trying to tell me that I needed to get started on it. The first chapter of this book was written the spring before Aunt Helen passed away that fall. A year later I lost my dad. I know now that God wanted me to have the chance of sharing some of it with them before He would call them home. After Aunt Helen died, dad never let me quit thinking about this dream. After he died, it seemed as though God would just randomly pick someone to remind me that I needed to continue working on it. I sometimes had to laugh when I would wonder if they were actually watching me from above, and then would go to our Heavenly Father and tell Him I was slipping, and would ask Him if He could please send me a reminder.

It has been over thirty years ago since my mother started telling me that I should share God's words with others, as to help encourage them in their own lives, as God had encouraged me. She was preparing me for this dream even then. But now I realize that I had to live this life to be able to share all that I have shared in this book. Back then, God already knew who He had planned to come into my life. He knew the relationships that I would have, and the friends that would take my hand on this journey. He knew the storms that I would encounter that would help my faith grow stronger than it ever could have without them. He had formed me like clay into His hands, and molded me into the person He wanted me to be. He had given me a goal to reach, and He had put a dream in my heart.

Right now, it is hard to explain the gratitude of thankfulness in my heart for what He has done for me. I thank Him for allowing my biological mother to unselfishly give me a better life than what she could have. I thank Him for giving to me parents that would help to nurture this dream He had for me. My heart is filled with joy and peace as I come to the end of this one particular journey.

I want to thank all of you who took the time to read this book. Life is so busy, and sometimes it's a task just to find a few minutes a day to sit and relax and spend time with God, and with yourself.

I pray that I have inspired you and filled you with hope. If you have read this, and can look back on your life and see that God truly held your hand your entire life, then I have accomplished everything I wanted too. If your trials seem a little lighter and your hope seems a little deeper, then God has truly given me the words that He knew you needed to hear. If it has made you laugh and cry both, then God has blessed you with allowing your emotions to pour forth.

This has been a dream come true for me, and I thank my Heavenly Father for sending me all the people and the tools I needed in order to complete this.

If the rains are pouring from the sky the day this book is published, I will not at all be surprised. I can just picture my mother and father, and Aunt Helen in Heaven, jumping up and down in excitement, shaking every raindrop from the clouds above.

I thought that losing my job was another trial in my life, but it turned out to be blessing. I have finally had more quiet time with the Lord, more time to spend in His presence, and more time to listen to Him. I have found the time to sit and put this whole book together and I praise Him for that. I know in my heart that this is what He had planned for me in the beginning.

Sometimes when a cloud covers the sky, and we see a storm approaching, it is only because there is a beautiful and promising rainbow just waiting to appear and decorate our life. There are times when the worst of storms can bring about the most beautiful rainbows. Doesn't that give you hope that the trials that we endure can be followed with a joy and peace that would not have been possible if we had not endured the storm first?

God has held my hand as we walked across the field of time. He sent me His most colorful rainbow to follow the storms in my life. He gave me His sunshine to warm my days with His love. He has undoubtedly helped me find the pot of gold at the end of the rainbow. This book, that He has helped me to write, is a rainbow in itself. It is His promise to me that He never let me down, and that He continued to guide me on this journey even when I had no idea where I was going.

I said before that whenever you see a rainbow in the sky, you know someday there will be another one. God has already put another dream in my heart of sharing another book with you. As long as His rainbows continue to cover the sky, I will never doubt what He can or will do in my life. I will wait patiently with an open heart to see where He will take me from here. This journey holds much happiness for me, for I know now that I have accomplished what He set out for me to do. I am now excited about doing even more.

I praise Him for everything. I thank Him for giving me this dream, and I thank all of you for sharing it with me. Take my hand, and let us continue walking together on this journey of faith. Always remember, that if a storm approaches, we will hold onto one another until the clouds go away, the high winds calm down, the sun comes out, and a rainbow decorates the sky. The blessings that await us are endless.

May God touch each one of you with His love, joy and peace, and may you always feel His presence surrounding you.

I know we will meet again someday, just as I know there will always be another rainbow.

Walking To Find The Rainbow

One day a little child had walked
What seemed like many miles,
She walked until she had to stop
And rest for a short while.

She had seen a rainbow in the sky
It's beauty touched her heart,
She wondered if it had an end
Or if it had a start.

She walked it seemed like endlessly
And suddenly she was grown,
She still kept searching for the end
Of the rainbow God had shown.

And then one day it suddenly came
This innocent thought so new,
She realized that the pot of gold
Had been there her whole life through.

For she had learned of God's joyous love
From the time her life began,
She knew that in the storms of life
He'd always held her hand.

She had searched for many endless years
To find the rainbows' end,
She did not know her treasure was
In her family and her friends.

I know the feeling this child had
For I am the child who walked the miles,
I now have found true love and peace
In the courage I found in trials.

Mary C. Cape-Juarez

I know God had a plan for me
He put a dream deep in my heart,
I'm able to touch the rainbow now
My spirit has a new start.

I will praise Him with glory forever
For all that He's given to me,
I'll share His love with everyone
And I'll trust Him faithfully.

GENESIS 9:13

"I SET MY BOW IN THE CLOUDS TO SERVE AS A SIGN OF THE COVENANT BETWEEN ME AND THE EARTH."

REFLECTION:

God sends us His rainbow to remind us of His faithfulness and love. What can we do to remind Him of ours?

Dear Heavenly Father

Thank You for Your beautiful rainbow that adorns the peaceful sky after the storms in life. Help it to always remind us that You will never abandon us. I ask that You will fill us with hope at the sight of it's magnificent colors, and that we will pass that hope onto others who are discouraged and frightened. You are our friend, and we know that You will always keep Your promise to us. In the most precious name of Your Son, Jesus Christ. Amen.

During my position as Spiritual Director of the Christ Renews His Parish team, I wrote prayers for my sisters in Christ in hopes they could find healing, guidance, and direction through our Lord.

Prayer For Forgiveness

Dear Heavenly Father

I come before you tonight with an open heart and soul. My heart is weeping because of the pain that I have caused you. You sent Your Son to die for me, but yet I still do things to hurt You. Tonight, I want to start all over again. I want to ask Your forgiveness for everytime in my life that I have went against your will. All of those sins from my past that I have buried inside of my being, that I was too ashamed to admit, I give them all to You tonight. I ask You to accept them, knowing that I realize now how much they hurt You. Cleanse me, My Lord and Savior, Son of my Heavenly Father, and heal me of my past. Forgive me for all the times I hurt You and the people I love. Help me to forgive all those people who have hurt me just as I know You have forgiven me. Purify my soul, that it may become as pure white as Your beautiful snow, and help me to learn how to keep it from ever being stained by sin again. Thank You for loving me as a sinner, and loving me unconditionally every day of my life. I praise You for Your loving mercy, and I ask for Your blessings of forgiveness and peace. In the most precious name of Your Son, Jesus Christ. Amen.

Prayer For Guidance

Dear Heavenly Father

I come to You today for guidance. I need Your help in leading me to do the job that You want me to do. I want to do Your will and not my own. Please bring out the talents in me that I did not know existed. Reassure me that with Your guidance, I have the capabilities of doing anything. Please encourage me if I get fearful, and feel incapable. Take my hand, and be my guidance. Let me feel Your presence in my heart, and to know Your will in my soul. I praise You and I love You. Thank You for always being there for me. In the most precious name of Your Son, Jesus Christ. Amen.

Prayer To Do Your Will

Dear Heavenly Father

We come to You today, and we ask Your blessing upon us. We want to do Your will, but we need You to guide us.

Let our feet walk us to the places where You lead us too.

Let our arms embrace the people You send to us who are in need of a hug, and secure arms around them.

Let our hands reach out to those who You are sending to us that need a hand to hold, and to walk beside them without letting go.

Let our lips whisper the words to a lonely heart that are words that come only from You.

Let our eyes give someone the look of hope that You are sending to them through us.

Let our smile be the smile that can remind someone that there is always happiness to be found.

Let our hearts be open to someone who needs some understanding and compassion in their lives.

Let our ears be open to what You are telling us, so that we may follow Your path that You are guiding us on.

Let us open our hearts and souls, so that we may let You pour out Your graces into the very deepest part of our being.

In the most precious name of Your Son, Jesus Christ. Amen.

Dear Heavenly Father

It was my dream to publish a book that would glorify Your name, and bring hearts and souls even closer to You. Thank You for letting me know Your will for me. Thank You for showing me the path to take to help make my dream come true, for leading me to the people who could help, for encouraging me as I traveled this journey, and for never letting me grow weary. Thank You for taking my hand and showing me the way. I praise You, Oh my Lord! In Jesus' name, I pray. Amen.

EPHESIANS 3:20-21

NOW TO HIM WHO IS ABLE TO ACCOMPLISH FAR MORE THAN ALL WE ASK OR IMAGINE, BY THE POWER AT WORK WITHIN US, TO HIM BE GLORY IN THE CHURCH AND IN CHRIST JESUS TO ALL GENERATIONS, FOREVER AND EVER. AMEN.

As I was working constantly at finishing up this book, I walked outside in the wee hours of the morning to get some fresh air. The full moon was brilliantly lighting up the entire sky. The very next night there was a beautiful rainbow that followed a small mist of rain. I knew in my heart that God was saying to me, "I told you that I would walk you through this, didn't I?" Through all of the hard work, and the nights when I was so discouraged I couldn't think straight, He truly had been there, and this was His way of letting me know.

Printed in the United States
51342LVS00005B/78

9 781420 887907